CASTLES
FROM THE AIR

An Aerial Portrait of Britain's Finest Castles

CASTLES FROM THE AIR

An Aerial Portrait of Britain's Finest Castles

PAUL JOHNSON

Photographs by Adrian Warren and Dae Sasitorn

BCL Press

First published in North America, Australia and New Zealand by BCL Press, 2006

Book Creation LLC, U.S.A.
Publishing Directors: Hal Robinson and John Kelly

Photography permissions:
© Photographs reproduced under licence from Last Refuge Ltd, Somerset,
www.lastrefuge.co.uk, unless otherwise stated in the acknowledgements on page 216.
All rights reserved.

Contributors:
David Halford, Paul Johnson, Elizabeth Loving, Dae Sasitorn, Adrian Warren

Editor: Lucilla Watson
Art Editor: Keith Miller
Design Consultant: Peter Laws
Proofreading: Alison Moore and Tamiko Rex

Photographs on pages:
1. *Camber Castle, East Sussex*
2. *Arundel Castle, West Sussex*
3. *Restormel Castle, Cornwall*

Front cover: *Ludlow Castle, Shropshire*
Back cover: *Castle Rising, Suffolk*
Spine: *Orford Castle, Suffolk*

Printed and bound in China

ISBN 1-932302-12-3

10 9 8 7 6 5 4 3 2 1

CONTENTS

✖

✖

FOREWORD

For most of us, a castle is a medieval fortress with formidable walls of stone, topped by battlements and surrounded by a moat. Such places of strength and refuge continue to capture our imagination, although castles are not only medieval masterpieces. As this book shows, fortified places have been part of the British landscape for millennia. They provide vital clues to the historical richness of our cultural heritage, whether they are complex systems of earthworks constructed more than 2,000 years ago by Iron Age communities, or whether they embody the more recent sophisticated splendour of great palace fortresses such as Windsor and Warwick.

When the first hunter-gatherers came to Britain more than half a million years ago, they encountered a land of plenty, rich in game. But even in those remote times there were skirmishes, using simple weapons, to steal tools, women, or to fight over the occupation of caves. Later, in the Neolithic period around 5,000 years ago, when people were beginning their first experiments with agriculture, the establishment of semi-permanent settlements required protective barriers against intruders and to corral animals. These Stone Age people built causewayed enclosures – large areas surrounded by earthworks of banks and ditches, probably fenced with wooden stakes. Built with the simplest of hand tools, these were immense undertakings, and perhaps the first 'castles' to adorn our landscape, which was very different at this time, and was almost entirely covered by forest. Gradually, as more settlers arrived, new skills and tools made it easier to clear the land for farming. As stone and bone tools gave way to those made from metal, the Neolithic period evolved into the Bronze Age and eventually the Iron Age. Earthwork fortifications became bigger and more complex, the larger ones home to communities of people with diverse technological skills.

When flying in our little plane over our rich green landscape, we try to imagine how it looked in those early times and why certain sites were selected. Remarkably, when seen from the air, all the clues are still there, some subtle, others more obvious, but all of them eroded by the course of time. Etched into the surface of the land are the remains of earthworks thousands of years old: barriers, hut circles, field systems, burial mounds, ancient trails, and stone circles and avenues of ritual significance. It is a delight to make these flights of discovery: after a while, we began to understand how these ancient settlements and fortifications fitted into the lie of the land, and sometimes were even able to predict accurately where they might be found.

With the invasion of the Romans came an impressive network of roads that reached the farthest corners of the land where fortresses of stone were built that must have seemed impregnable. After the Romans left in the early 5th century, incoming Germanic settlers established communities and later built their own forts on steep-sided mounds as defences against Norse invaders. The conquering Normans, too, embarked on a spree of castle building, sometimes on previously occupied sites where communities grew up around their strongholds. Far from being mute witnesses of history, all of these types of 'castles' have influenced the growth and layout of the villages, towns and cities that we inhabit today.

Paul Johnson's authoritative text and our accompanying aerial photographs tell the story of British castles as paramount examples of grand design, from their beginnings in prehistory right the way through to their renaissance in the 19th century. This book explains how castle builders were able to take advantage of the topography of the landscape so that their fortresses could perform their role as centres of political and military power. Despite the wanton destruction of so many during the 17th-century Civil War, the castles of England, Scotland and Wales today form one of the most diverse and important collections of national monuments worldwide. Aerial photography allows us to appreciate castles in a way that their original builders could never have foreseen, as well as offering insights into their strategic design and significance.

Adrian Warren and Dae Sasitorn
Somerset, 31 May 2006

Eilean Donan Castle, Scotland.

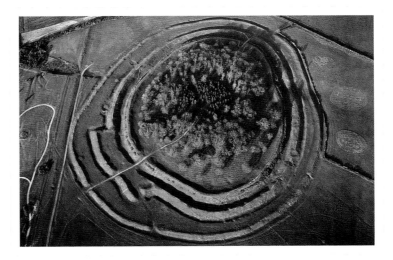

HIGH DEFENDED PLACES

*'The Britons apply the term "stronghold" to densely
wooded spots fortified with a rampart and trench to which
they retire in order to escape the attacks of invaders.
The [stronghold] was of great natural strength and
excellently fortified.'*

JULIUS CAESAR, THE CONQUEST OF GAUL (52–51 BC)

It is from the air that the most spectacular of Britain's ancient hillforts can best be appreciated. With their astonishing ramparts of high banks and deep ditches, and their complex system of gateways, skilfully designed to put attackers at a disadvantage, these hillforts remodelled the landscape. Built from the late Bronze Age, hillforts became a feature of the landscape of southern Britain in the increasingly warlike Iron Age. But, against superior Roman forces, hillforts were powerless. Imprints of the new Roman order, reflected in buildings with quadrilateral lines, are clearly visible in aerial views of towns such as Wroxeter and Canterbury, and in the famous legionary fortress of Housesteads, on Hadrian's Wall. As the Roman Empire declined, Britain faced a fresh wave of invaders, the Saxons, who guarded the frontiers of their new territory by building spectacular earthworks like Wansdyke. In rare cases, traces of all these phases of early British history are preserved at a single site, such as Old Sarum, which was occupied from the Iron Age to Saxon times. Again, only in aerial photographs is this historical continuity fully revealed.

ABOVE: *The wooded hilltop of Badbury Rings, an Iron Age fort just outside Wimborne Minster, in Dorset, rises 300 ft (91 m) above the sharply etched circles of its defensive banks and ditches. Probably destroyed by Roman troops in AD 44, Badbury was in use from at least 1000 BC.*

LEFT: *Dating from c.200 BC, the remains of a once-mighty Iron Age hillfort cling to the summit of Hereford Beacon, in the Malvern Hills, some 10 miles (16 km) south of Worcester. The site, which covers 32 acres (13 ha), was shrewdly chosen by its inhabitants: the 1,115 ft (340 m) beacon controls a pass at the southern tip of the Malvern Hills.*

ANCIENT BRITAIN

The earliest military defences built in Britain were the late Bronze Age and Iron Age hillforts. They were built over a period of 1,000 years before the birth of Christ, and in huge numbers. About 2,520 are known to archaeologists today, but their distribution is uneven. In West and South Wales, in Cornwall and in most of Devon, hillforts are very common and small. They are also widespread, and small in size, in the area of the Scottish Borders, and around the firths of Forth and Tay. In areas farther east, and especially in southeastern England, hillforts are much fewer, but larger; and there are also innumerable unfortified enclosures. This suggests that, in the southeast, an organized social system developed relatively early, which stamped out the casual raiding of farms and flocks, and imposed a degree of civil peace. In these areas, the largest hillforts were almost certainly regional capitals, and seats of government and authority. In most of the west and the north, where inter-communal and inter-tribal raiding continued into historic times, farmers had no alternative but to build permanent defences.

Almost all hillforts were built on high ground, with one or more surrounding ditches. The earliest hillforts, many of which predate the Iron Age, were defended by a single rampart – either a stone wall, or a bank and ditch. The first fully developed Iron Age culture appeared in Britain around 600 BC, gradually spreading from the southeast and reaching the remoter parts of the west and north around 400–300 BC. A more sophisticated Iron Age culture penetrated southeast Britain around 250 BC, and brought with it the sling. This revolution in military technology led to the development of hillforts with two or more concentric banks and ditches, set close together, giving a formidable advantage to defenders equipped with slings. Then, about 100 years before the coming of the Romans, Belgic invaders, famed for their use of metal, fine pottery and coinage, reached southeast England. Their forts, larger and fewer in number, had highly complicated systems of linear earthworks.

Almost all hillforts were built to be inhabited. In Scotland, however, many were used only when herds were moved to summer upland pastures. Most hillforts were, in effect, fortified farmsteads – single enclosures large enough for only one family plus their slaves and dependants. But some have much more elaborate defences, and enclosed a larger area, even though they were still intended for a single family group. These forts often have a small, inner enclosure, surrounded by wide spaces protected by one or more shallow ramparts. In these, the family lived in the inner enclosure, and cattle were protected in the outer ones. A few forts housed the equivalent of entire villages, even towns. Some, such as Bindon Hill, in Dorset, and Hengistbury Head, in Hampshire, were enormous. Such huge forts may have been fortified invasion centres or trading bases. Large hillforts were also used for great tribal gatherings.

The masterpiece of Iron Age military architecture was Maiden Castle, in Dorset. Using picks fashioned from antlers and shovels made from the shoulderblades of oxen, thousands must have toiled on this work of vast size and complexity. In its final form it bears the stamp of the technology of the Belgic settlers, of the 1st century BC, though its origins go back 3,000 years earlier.

No British hillfort was built to withstand a formal siege in the Roman sense; they simply offered protection against raiding and tribal warfare. Generally with no provision for storing large quantities of food and water, Iron Age hillforts were not logistically equipped to withstand blockade. The Britons also had no answer to Roman siege engines, heavy firepower, discipline and method, and their hillforts quickly fell to the Romans. Thus the majority of hillforts went out of use in the 1st century AD.

ROMAN BRITAIN

The Romans gave Britain the elements of a uniform, centrally directed military system. Rome's military power was based on the legion, a body of troops formed and trained to seek out and destroy all enemy forces. Fixed defences were established primarily to enable the legionary army to work more efficiently, and their importance was thus secondary. Even so, the Romans were innovators in castle and fortress building. They were the first to introduce defences of a standard design. These were chiefly rectangular, often with rounded corners, and the buildings within were laid out to a regular pattern. They were not so much castles as fortified bases, from which units of

ABOVE: *Seen from the air in late summer, the broken granite ramparts of Chun Castle, near St Just, not far from the coast of Cornwall, stand out clearly against the surrounding bracken and burnt heather. Constructed some 2,500 years ago, this was a fortified farmstead. Much of the stone was later removed from the site for use as building material, but the upstanding lintels of the entrance still survive.*

RIGHT: *With a rampart and a ditch, Mam Tor, in the Derbyshire Peak District west of Sheffield, bears the characteristic marks of an Iron Age hillfort, and at 1,700 ft (520 m), it is the second-highest in the British Isles. The hillfort superseded a late Bronze Age settlement, where more than 100 platforms were cut into the rock to provide the foundations for huts.*

varying sizes operated. Indeed, they were essentially a development of the entrenched camp: all Roman units were trained to set up defences of ditches and wooden stockades wherever they happened to camp. Such camps were laid out to standard patterns. In all essentials, a Roman legionary fortress, or for that matter a fortified town, was simply a permanent version of the nocturnal stockade.

But, although Rome kept huge numbers of professional soldiers under arms, there was constant financial pressure, over so large an empire, to spread military manpower as thinly as possible; and it was this consideration that led to the construction of fixed lines. Of these the most important was Hadrian's Wall, built in the early 2nd century AD, roughly on a line from Carlisle to Newcastle, over a distance of 73 miles (117 km). Like most other permanent Roman military

constructions, it has a concrete core with stone facings. The standard thickness is 7 ft 6 in (2.3 m), broadening to 9 ft 6 in (3 m) in parts, and the average height of the wall walk is about 15 ft (4.5 m). On the lower stretches there is a deep ditch with a level terrace, or berm, between the ditch and the wall; and in addition, on the 'pacified' side of the wall, there is the so-called *vallum*, a ditch whose precise purpose is still debated, but which seems most likely to have been a form of rearward defence. The wall is equipped with 16 forts, on the standard Roman model, at 4-mile (2.5-km) intervals; and at every Roman mile there is a milecastle, projecting inwards from the wall, and measuring 60 by 70 ft (18 by 21 m) internally. One of the main forts, Housesteads, on the most impressive section of the wall, has been fully excavated.

Clearly the wall was of no great value against a massed attack, even of savages, since there were no stairways to the top other than at the stations. It was designed, rather, to stop routine infiltration by raiding parties and, in the case of mass attacks, to gain time for an outflanking movement by Roman troops issuing from the north gates of the forts. In short, it was a tripwire and a series of bases. As such, it probably served its purpose of cutting down the total manpower needed to man the northern frontier, especially since it was linked by semaphore to the main northern base in York. But not all Roman governors were content with it. In the reign of Antoninus Pius (142–3), the so-called Antonine Wall was built to the north, on a line from old Kilpatrick, on the Clyde, to Bo'ness, on the Forth. This, too, was a continuous line, dotted with 19 forts at intervals of 2 miles (3 km).

(continued on page 17)

LEFT: *The figure of the Westbury White Horse is cut into the chalky hillside just below the great platform of Bratton Castle, a hillfort dating from the 1st millennium BC. Bratton Castle, in Wiltshire, lies northwest of the Bronze Age masterpiece of Stonehenge, and commands spectacular views for miles all around.*

BELOW: *The stronghold of Uffington Castle, 20 miles (32 km) west of Wallingford, in southern Oxfordshire, overlooks the Ridgeway – the ancient trackway that crosses lowland Britain from Overton Hill, in Wiltshire, to Ivinghoe Beacon, in Buckinghamshire. The hillfort dates back 3,000 years, and the area is rich in prehistoric remains, including the strangely stylized figure of a horse cut into the chalk hillside just to the east of the ramparts.*

MAIDEN CASTLE

DORSET

Maiden Castle is located 2 miles (3 km) south of Dorchester, Dorset, off the A354.

HISTORICAL IMPORTANCE

The Roman invasion of Britain began in AD 43 with a landing on the southeast coast. The Roman advance westwards met with resistance from the Britons, and the great hillfort of Maiden Castle – the tribal centre of the Durotriges – was attacked by Vespasian, at the head of a legion. Although it was defended by a formidable series of ramparts and ditches, the hillfort was impotent against Roman siege technology. The legionaries used large catapults, known as *ballistae*, to hurl stones and metal bolts over the ramparts, and the hillfort was taken. Maiden Castle was abandoned, although a small Romano-British temple was later built in one corner. Excavations at the fort revealed a war cemetery that contained the bones of some of its defenders, including one whose skull had been pierced by a bolt from a *ballista*, and another whose spine had an arrowhead embedded in it.

NOTABLE FEATURES

Viewed from the air, Maiden Castle's massive proportions are immediately apparent, with three concentric lines of banks and ditches and a complex system of gateways at its eastern and western ends. Originally occupied by late Stone Age farmers, the area of the fort was extended in about 350 BC to cover 45 acres (18 ha), and elaborate earthworks were built to provide a defended settlement for several hundred inhabitants and their livestock. The soil dug out to make the ditches was thrown up to form a series of huge banks, topped by a wooden palisade, that encircled the site. The gateways, built of timber and stone, were deliberately offset so as to confuse attackers. In the Iron Age – a time of inter-tribal warfare – the hillfort gave its inhabitants the advantage of a strategic stronghold in the surrounding territory.

But, stretching for 36 miles (58 km), it was much shorter, and of inferior construction – of clay and sods laid like bricks – with a heavy stone foundation 14 ft (4 m) wide. It was only 10 ft (3 m) high, with sloping sides, a wall walk 6 ft (2 m) wide, and a fort-foot ditch; some of the forts have stone walls, but others are of clay with turf ramparts.

In addition to pressure on their northern land defences, the Romans had to cope, from the mid-3rd century, with seaborne raids from Saxony and other territories beyond their Continental lines. The threat became so serious that the Romans completely restructured their military organization in Britain, and created a new command of seaward defences, under the Count of the Saxon Shore. This coastal command, in turn, undertook the most extensive programme of military works carried out in Britain until comparatively modern times. There was a triple-layered infrastructure. At one level, there was a series of signal stations, set on the main headlands of the eastern and southern coasts and at selected points in the west. They have been identified at Scarborough, Goldsborough, Huncliffe and Filey, and there were undoubtedly many others along the exposed coasts of the North Sea and the eastern English Channel.

Each consisted of a tall stone tower, 43 ft (13 m) square and 100 ft (30 m) high, surmounted by a semaphore apparatus and a fire-lantern. Below, a battlemented wall enclosed a courtyard. These stations served to give advance warning of raids. The aim, again, was to stretch the available manpower as far as possible.

At a second level there were a number of small forts, chiefly on the western coasts – where Roman units were few and far between, and where the threat of mass attack from the sea was much less serious. Two such were the fort at Caernarfon, controlling the western end of the Menai Straits, and Caer Gibi (or Gybi) near Holyhead. The latter is comparatively well preserved. Three of its sides stand to the height of the wall walk, 12 ft (3.5 m) above the ground. But it was a modest construction, less than 1 acre (0.5 ha) in area. Its concrete wall, faced with stone and bonded with flat stone courses, was 5 ft 6 in (1.7 m) thick, with cylindrical towers in each corner, and a gateway in the north and south walls.

At the third level were really massive fortifications, built in south-eastern Britain to bear the main brunt of the Saxon sea-offensive. These fortifications were much stronger than the forts built to house

(continued on page 21)

LEFT: *Excavations on the top of Eggardon Hillfort, 10 miles (17 km) west of Dorchester, Dorset, revealed storage pits and the remains of circular houses dating from the late Iron Age. Today, a parish boundary, clearly visible from the air, runs through the centre of the settlement. In Saxon times, the hillfort was used for meetings of the local administration – the 'hundred moot'.*

ABOVE: *Cley Hill, one of a series of Iron Age hilltop sites in Wiltshire, lies almost 20 miles (33 km) due west of Stonehenge. The concentric lines of ramparts and ditches hug the contours of the hill, which at 800 ft (245 m) high, provides an all-round panoramic view. In recent years the fort has acquired a reputation as a good place to spot unidentified flying objects.*

BROCH OF GURNESS

ORKNEY

The Broch of Gurness is located 14 miles (23 km)
northwest of Kirkwall, Orkney, on the A966.

HISTORICAL IMPORTANCE

Brochs – tall, drystone circular towers dating from the Iron Age –
are found only in Scotland. The Broch of Gurness forms the core
of a village with compact stone houses surrounding the central
tower, the whole settlement being encircled by protective ditches
and banks. Gurness is one of six brochs on the northeast coast of
Mainland, the largest of the Orkney Islands. It looks out over
Eynhallow Sound to the south coast of Rousay, where at least five
more are situated. Coastal erosion has washed away part of each
settlement, but the large number of known brochs here indicates
the sea's importance for transport and trade in what was possibly
the hub of activity in Orkney around 200 BC. The Broch of
Gurness's size and the extent of its defences suggest that it was
inhabited by one of the most powerful families in the area.

NOTABLE FEATURES

The focus of the site is the remains of the broch's tower, which was
solidly constructed, with large foundations on a raised platform.
Leading from the two entrances to the broch itself – one located
within its massive walls – is a causeway, which runs down through
the settlement, through two gateways and across the outer
defensive ditches. Even today, this is reminiscent of a processional
route: it was clearly designed to awe the visitor and give a sense of
the inhabitants' grandeur. The timber fittings of the broch and its
houses rotted away long ago, but enough remains of the stone
fixtures – hearths, cupboards and storage pits – to suggest how life
was lived on this windswept coast. Intriguingly, remnants of
Roman pottery that were found here indicate that there was
contact between the Orcadians and the inhabitants of southern
Britain in the 1st century AD.

The hillfort of Scratchbury, northwest of Heytesbury, Wiltshire, dates from the 1st century BC. Covering more than 35 acres (15 ha), its defences enclose an earlier, much smaller site. Excavations of the seven barrows within the fort revealed cremation burials and artefacts of bronze and amber.

cohorts, or even whole legions, and they have withstood the assaults of time and history to an amazing degree. Their ditches were very wide and deep, and their walls spectacularly high and broad. Two, Pevensey and Lymne, were irregular; but most were of the standard rectangular shape. Unlike the usual Roman defended town, they had few gates and those few were narrow and easy to defend. The towers, too, projected outwards, helping the *ballistae* to cover the walls in between. They were designed to make the maximum use of Roman superiority in firepower.

Among the outstanding examples of the Saxon Shore defences were Burgh in Suffolk, Bradwell-juxta-Mare in Essex, Reculver, Richborough and Lympne in Kent, Pevensey in Sussex, and Portchester in Hampshire. These were all huge forts, with walls 25 ft (8 m) high and 12–15 ft (4–5 m) thick that were impervious to any artillery the Saxons possessed: their only hope of a successful assault was to go for the gates. But of course the Romans built these forts chiefly to concentrate troops and supplies. They were bases for flying columns of cavalry, and of infantry transported rapidly to beach-heads by sea, as well as secure areas where vast numbers of local inhabitants, plus their cattle and valuables, could be harboured.

Thanks to those massive walls we still have a good general idea of what these supercastles looked like when they were in their prime. The best-preserved example of all is Portchester. It was kept in good repair during the Middle Ages (as was Pevensey), and fortunately was not slighted in the 1640s. The walls follow the entire perimeter, up to a height of 20 ft (6 m). They are made of flint, 10 ft (3 m) thick, bonded with courses of brick and stone slate. Every inch of perimeter wall was covered by circular wall-towers, one on each corner and four on each side. But there were only two gateways, instead of the customary four or six, and each was strongly defended.

As at Pevensey, the Normans reoccupied the fort, making use of the perimeter wall but building a castle in the northwest corner. The perimeter then became a sort of outer bailey, and it is clear that the Normans did not possess the manpower to occupy the whole length of the wall in strength. Hence the need for a castle keep, something with which Roman forts were not equipped. How many men manned these forts in Roman times? For places like Burgh and Portchester, it cannot have been fewer than 1,000. And herein lay the ultimate weakness of the Roman military system: manning their defences, however cunningly contrived, placed ultimately unsupportable burdens on resources. The forts of the Saxon Shore were invulnerable when garrisoned at the planned level. But the day came when all Roman forces had to be withdrawn, and then the system became unworkable. Pevensey was taken by assault in 491, something that had never happened under the Romans. Other forts fell to the Saxons without a fight.

(continued on page 24)

HOUSESTEADS FORT

NORTHUMBERLAND

*Housesteads Fort is located on Hadrian's Wall,
4 miles (6 km) from Bardon Mill, Northumberland.*

HISTORICAL IMPORTANCE

Housesteads Fort formed part of the support system of Roman forts, milecastles and turrets that were built at regular intervals along Hadrian's Wall. The fort was designed to hold about 1,000 troops and its remains are the most extensive of any in Britain. The wall, 75 miles (120 km) long, was built on the orders of the Emperor Hadrian after he inspected his northernmost province in AD 122. It was intended both as a frontier and as a means of suppressing fierce local resistance. Occupied for almost 300 years, Housesteads Fort was also the focus for a substantial settlement of civilians, most of them traders, craftsmen and retired soldiers, that grew up outside its gates. Since the settlement was unprotected, its extent indicates that the garrison at Housesteads was successful in helping to keep the peace in this rugged and beautiful area at the very edge of the Roman Empire.

NOTABLE FEATURES

This aerial view shows the precision of the fort's layout, which was based on that of Roman tented camps. The *principia*, the headquarters building at the centre, housed a shrine for the legionary standards and a statue of the emperor, and contained administrative offices. Centurions' meetings were held here. Next door were the fort commandant's house and the granaries. These were roofed in stone as a precaution against incendiary attack, and to protect the walls from rain were projecting eaves supported on buttresses. Each barrack block was divided into ten rooms that were partitioned into sleeping quarters and storage areas, with two larger rooms at the end for officers. The fort had four gateways, each flanked by a guardroom, and in its southeast corner is a latrine, one of the few found along Hadrian's Wall.

In fact, the Romano-British, pushed steadily westwards by the advancing Germanic invaders in the 5th and 6th centuries, were almost wholly unable to make use of the Roman military structures, and fared better when they fell back on the traditional hillforts of their race. There is evidence that many of these came back into use after the Romans left and, at least in the southwest, some earthworks were refortified. This seems to have occurred, for example, at South Cadbury, in Somerset, and at Castle Dore, in Cornwall. In a few cases new hillforts were built. Thus the large fort of Dinas Emrys in Gwynedd, traditionally associated with the Romano-British cavalry commander Ambrosius Aurelianus, has defence works that are dated fairly confidently in the mid-5th century. In Scotland, Iron Age forts of the nuclear type (built on rock or headlands, and similar) remained in use until the 8th century. One of the last of these, Dunadd, in Argyll, was captured by the Picts as late as 736.

These Scottish redoubts were effectively the final functioning of a military tradition going back nearly four millennia. It is significant that the Angles, Saxons and Jutes, as they settled over England proper, rejected the tradition as archaic. They had their own military traditions, which were quite different. One was the construction of frontier lines, no doubt originally based on Roman models. The largest, Offa's Dyke, runs for 120 miles (195 km) from the Wye to the Dee estuary, marking the border between Mercia and Wales. It consists of a high rampart, with a ditch on the western side, and in its northern section it is reinforced for 36 miles (60 km) by a parallel barrier known as Wat's Dyke. This barrier performed roughly the same functions, in a more primitive manner, as Hadrian's Wall. Such frontier defences were common in Anglo-Saxon England, though most have long since disappeared. A remarkable survivor is Wansdyke, which runs for 60 miles (97 km) from Somerset to Hampshire.

ANGLO-SAXON AND NORMAN BRITAIN

The Anglo-Saxons also used or built strongpoints, though here the picture is more confused. There is some evidence that, for a time at least, they took over the remains of Roman fortresses, as at Colchester. But in general these new settlers in England did not occupy Roman towns and their defences. The Anglo-Saxons were peasants and forest-dwellers, who built essentially in timber. Yet they could use stone, too, in a masterly fashion. Since they could build stone churches of high quality, we must assume they could, and did, build stone castles, though few traces remain. The Anglo-Saxon Chronicle records that the Saxons fortified Bamburgh with a wall in 547; and Bede, writing about 630, refers to other castles in Northumbria. In Cornwall, it is likely that Tintagel, originally fortified in prehistoric times, and almost certainly defended by Romano-British soldiers after the Romans' departure, was refortified and remained in being

LEFT: *Richborough Castle, on the Kent coast, has a double significance in the history of Roman Britain. In AD 43, it was the first landing site for invasion forces, but around 270 it was rebuilt as one of 12 forts raised to counter the increasing menace of Saxon raids in the southeast. The large cross inside the fort was the base for a massive 1st-century Roman triumphal arch.*

ABOVE: *The outline of Chesters Cavalry Fortress, on Hadrian's Wall, is clearly visible in this aerial view, together with the stone abutment of the Roman bridge. The garrison baths – which form some of the most extensive Roman remains in Britain – are located outside the fort, close to the river. Excavations carried out in the 19th century revealed the oak door to the fort's strongroom still in place.*

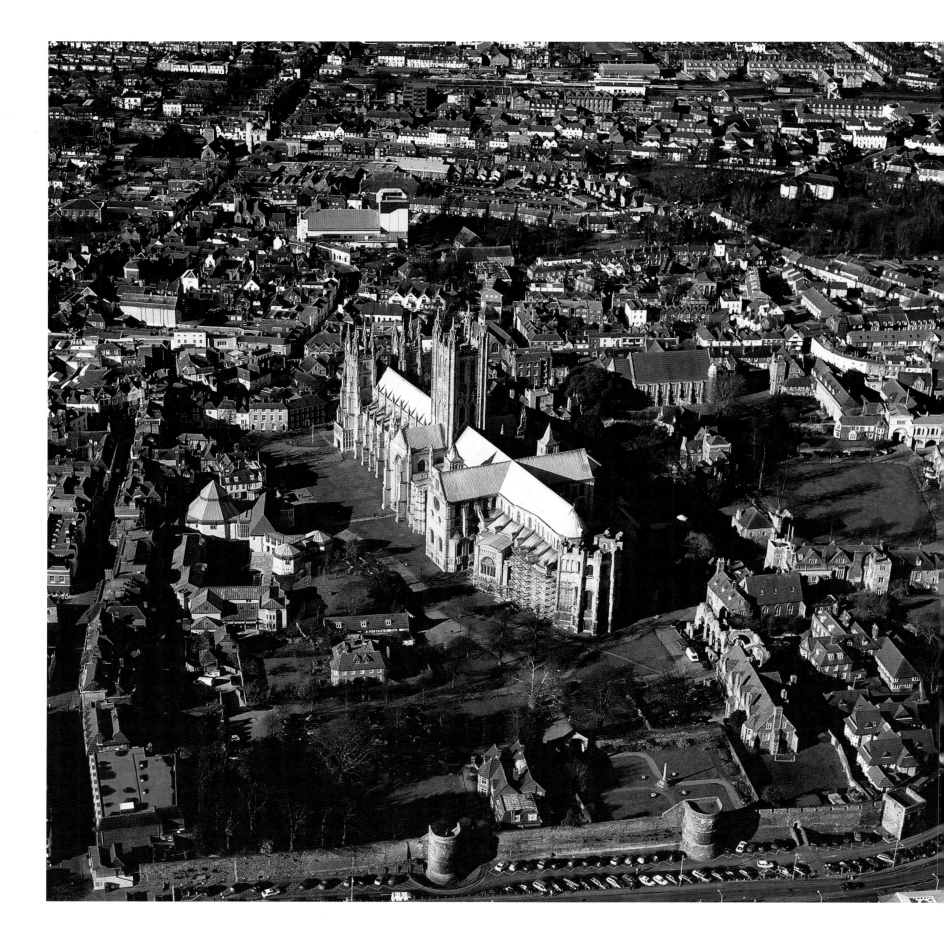

during the Anglo-Saxon period. In most cases, however, we cannot trace Anglo-Saxon forts and fortified buildings, either because they were made of wood, or because their remains are buried under later structures. Two exceptions are the fortified royal palaces of Yeavering, a *villa regalis* in Northumberland, and Cheddar, in Somerset. There must have been many more of these princely houses at one time, each defended by a powerful palisade, with watchtowers, a ditch and, where possible, a moat. But these palaces were akin to the fortified manor houses of the later Middle Ages, designed to protect their inhabitants against intruders and casual marauders, rather than regular armies. However, as the threat to western Europe from Scandinavia increased, more substantial fortifications came into use again.

The inspiration came from northwest France and Flanders. From 862, the Frankish king Charles the Bald ordered the building of powerful forts against the Normans, and instituted a system whereby private landowners were licensed to build castles of their own. Seven years later, he commanded the fortification of all towns between the Seine and Loire. During the next decade, the Saxons of Wessex began to adopt the Frankish system of defence. In 878, King Alfred built the first new fort at Athelney, as a prelude to his victory over the Danes at Edington. Their raids were then switched to France, and Alfred used the breathing-space to build fortified towns with permanent garrisons. Thus systematic fortification began in 879. These new fortified burghs of Alfred's were sited on rivers that served as Danish entry-routes, sometimes on both banks. A Danish base on the Lea was blocked by two forts built by Alfred in 895; and the twin-fort technique was used at Bedford, Buckingham, Hertford, and Stamford.

Although Alfred began the refortification of England, the bulk of the work was the responsibility of his successors in the early 10th century, Edward the Elder and Aethelflaed, the Lady of Mercia. Aethelflaed built the fortified towns of Bridgnorth, Stafford, Tamworth, Warwick, Chirbury, Eddisbury and Runcorn, with three others not yet identified. Her brother Edward built Hertford, Buckingham, Bedford, Stamford and Nottingham, and refortified Towcester, Huntingdon, Colchester and London. Such forts were not built to a rigid pattern, but as local conditions permitted. Hence, at Lydford in Devon, at Christchurch in Hampshire and at Burpham near Arundel, earthworks were thrown up across a promontory, in accordance with prehistoric methods of fortification. At Bath, Winchester, Portchester, Chichester and Exeter, the Roman walls were repaired and rearranged. In Chester, too, the walls were rebuilt. Wareham, Cricklade and Wallingford were built on new sites, but on a rectangular Roman pattern. Throughout Wessex, Surrey and Sussex, no village was farther than 20 miles (30 km) from a manned fort. Most defences were in timber. Hence in many cases the sites have vanished without trace. In the great majority of cases, Norman castles were superimposed on Anglo-Saxon defended towns.

The legacy of the Roman presence in Britain can sometimes still be clearly detected in the layout of towns and cities. Built on the site of an earlier British tribal settlement, Canterbury, 10 miles (16 km) west of Richborough Castle, was an administrative centre in Roman times. The city walls were built in the 3rd century, and the later medieval walls followed the line of the Roman defences.

There is plainly an important difference between Anglo-Saxon fortified towns and the Norman-style castle of the 11th century. All Anglo-Saxon defences, like those of the Romans, were essentially communal and royal. But in the confused conditions of Charles the Bald's day, central authority had been obliged to delegate much of the defence of the realm to the private lord, who acted independently. The king did this with reluctance, and retained the theory that, in strict legal terms, all fortresses were his unless he specifically ruled otherwise. His decree of 862 permitted the private construction of 'castles, forts and hedgeworks' under licence. Two years later he commanded them to be destroyed. In 869, the military situation having deteriorated again, he ordered their reconstruction. So it went on: the military necessities of the realm competing with the monarch's desire to keep all fixed defences under his control, or to demolish them.

As the Normans became settled and civilized on the Continent, they met the same problem themselves. By 950 or so, mention is made in northern France and soon after in Anjou, of individual 'towers'. Some of these were of stone, and thus fire-resistant. The Danes made their contribution by throwing up earthworks of the motte type (a central mound) as a foundation for timber buildings. At all events, castles began to spring up in Normandy from the time that William I inherited the duchy in 1035. On these frontier districts, viscounts were in charge and they naturally built the latest defences – the origins of the motte-and-bailey castle. But the duke decreed that no such castles could be built without ducal licence, and that he might take possession of any castle whenever he thought fit.

The problem in England was much less acute. In theory, there were no private castles at all in Anglo-Saxon times, and no licensing system until the 12th century. But as a political connection developed between England and Normandy, so the Norman-type castle and the principle of private ownership were introduced. In 1051, the Anglo-Saxon Chronicle records that 'the foreigners [Normans] had built a castle in Herefordshire'. Also in connection with the Normans, the Chronicle mentions 'Pentecost's castle' and 'Robert's castle'.

This, then, is documentary evidence of three castles (at least) built by Normans in pre-Conquest England. There are reasonable grounds for believing that 'aenne castel on Herefordscire' was on the site of Hereford itself. It may have been built in 1048, an early example of the motte-and-bailey type. Pentecost's Castle has been identified with Ewyas Harold Castle in Herefordshire. It is built on a spur, a standard motte-and-bailey castle, but with no sign of a ditch on the bailey side. It was one of the earliest Norman fortifications on the Welsh borders.

Robert's Castle, also in occupation in 1051–2, has been identified with Clavering, in Essex. It seems to have consisted of a rectangular moated enclosure with outer mounds and banks. But there is also a fourth castle, called Richard's Castle, 5 miles (8 km) south of Ludlow, in Herefordshire. It consisted of a motte and bailey with a strong counterscarp bank and an outer bank and ditch.

Hence, in three, very likely four (and perhaps more) cases, the Norman invasion of Anglo-Saxon England was foretold by the erection of alien, privately held castles, the mark of a completely new social and military structure. It was to be imposed on the entire country by force.

ABOVE: *Battlesbury Hillfort, just outside Warminster, is one of a concentration of Iron Age tribal strongholds on the western edges of Wiltshire. The lines of its ramparts and complex entrances are clearly visible from the air. The archaeology in southern Britain's hillforts has often been compromised by agriculture, especially ploughing.*

RIGHT: *Perched high above the Dee Valley, in North Wales, Castell Dinas Bran overlooks the river and the town of Llangollen. The remains of an Iron Age hillfort can be also made out. Located less than 5 miles (8 km) from Offa's Dyke, the 8th-century earthwork that marks the ancient boundary between Wales and England, this was an area of strategic importance, and a later stone castle was built on the Iron Age site.*

Figsbury Ring, some 4 miles (6 km) northeast of Salisbury, Wiltshire, has the familiar bank-and-ditch defensive circle that is typical of Iron Age hillforts, as well as an inner, circular ditch whose function is not known. The hillfort, which covers more than 15 acres (6 ha), may have been inhabited only in times of danger.

Danebury Ring, 5 miles (8 km) south of Andover, Hampshire, was a defended Iron Age settlement from the middle of the 1st millennium BC probably until the Roman period. With ramparts enclosing an area of 13 acres (5 ha), the hillfort could accommodate an estimated 300 people. While they are very impressive from the ground, from the air Danebury's high defensive banks and deep ditches are largely hidden by dense woodland.

LEFT: *The hour-glass-shaped enclosure of Beacon Hillfort, which lies near the Hampshire–Berkshire border, 5 miles (8 km) south of Newbury, contains clear traces of Iron Age habitation. Twenty circles, the vestiges of circular huts, together with the remains of storage pits are scattered across the 12-acre (5-ha) enclosure.*

ABOVE: *Old Sarum lies just north of its successor, the city of Salisbury. With huge Iron Age ramparts that encircle the remains of a medieval castle and cathedral, Old Sarum is a good example of historical continuity. There is evidence of Roman settlement here, and after the site was abandoned, it was reoccupied by the Saxons in about AD 900.*

The tribal stronghold of Hod Hill, 15 miles (24 km) northeast of Dorchester, is the largest Iron Age hillfort in Dorset. This aerial view shows the remains of its hut circles, as well as the Roman fort built about AD 44. A considerable number of ballista bolts were found around one large hut in particular, possibly that of the tribal chief.

Roman Wroxeter, just southeast of the modern town of Shrewsbury, Shropshire, had its origins in the legionary fortress that was built as part of the Romans' military campaign against the native Welsh. The later city – substantial by Roman standards and covering some 200 acres (80 ha) – was a planned civilian settlement with a forum and shops, and public baths that included an exercise hall and an open-air swimming pool.

ABOVE: *The stepped ramparts of the Iron Age hillfort at Cadbury rise to 500 ft (150 m). From the summit of the hillfort, Glastonbury, some 12 miles (19 km) to the southeast, can be seen. Cadbury has long been linked to King Arthur and is believed by some to be the site of the legendary Camelot.*

RIGHT: *The huge linear earthwork of Wansdyke, with its deep ditch, ran west to east across country possibly extending from Portishead, on the coast of Somerset, to a point south of Marlborough, in Wiltshire. This photograph shows the stretch of the earthwork to the northeast of Devizes, Wiltshire. Like Offa's Dyke, it probably served a dual purpose: as a boundary and as a defence. It was built some time between AD 400 and 700 after the Roman withdrawal, Britain's so-called Dark Ages.*

CONQUEST & CONTROL

'The king ... fortified strategic sites against enemy attacks.
For the fortifications called castles (castella) by the
Normans were scarcely known in the English provinces, so
that the English could only put up a weak resistance...'

ORDERICUS VITALIS, ECCLESIASTICAL HISTORY, 12TH CENTURY

The Norman Conquest introduced a radically new phase of castle building to England. This began with the motte-and-bailey castle, built initially, and somewhat hastily, of wood, but later of durable, fireproof stone. Seen from the air, these great Norman castles reveal the genius of their architecture. They are most often set on high ground – either a hill or an artificial mound – and consist of a long curtain wall encircling a square, circular or polygonal keep. According to the Domesday Book, at least 49 such castles had been built within 20 years of the Battle of Hastings. They were fairly evenly distributed over southern England, but were concentrated along the south and east coast, and along the borders with Wales and with Scotland. Henry II inaugurated another great wave of castle building in England, which was continued by his successors. As Crusaders brought new ideas back from the Holy Land, so the design of castles developed, their defences becoming more elaborate, as many of these aerial views clearly show. Concessions to comfort were also starting to be made, initiating the gradual evolution of the castle as a stern, strictly practical place of defence to a comfortable residence where the pleasures of life might be enjoyed.

ABOVE: *The scant remains of Tenby Castle in South Wales, built in the 12th century, perch on the headland that overlooks the harbour and the town. In the 19th century, a fort was built on a rocky island offshore.*

LEFT: *Bamburgh Castle, captured and refortified by William II in 1093, sprawls along a basalt outcrop on the coast of Northumbria. The core of its fortifications was the great stone keep, a characteristic element of Norman military architecture that became a familiar part of the landscape in the years following the Conquest.*

THE NORMAN YOKE

The Normans were organizers and militarists of genius. They did not invent armoured cavalry; nor did they invent fortified bases; and they certainly did not invent the basic concept of feudalism, which was the holding of land from a superior lord in exchange for knight-service. But they were the first to combine all three and regulate the resulting system in a thoroughly businesslike manner. On a regular battlefield and in open warfare, their heavy cavalry gave them an immense advantage, even against ferocious and well-disciplined infantry like Harold Godwinson's *housecarls*. Armour and horsepower had won the Battle of Hastings. But what turned their victories into conquests was the speed and skill with which they erected castles, to consolidate their territorial gains and to terrorize and demoralize the subject population. This was the essence of the 'Norman Yoke' – part of English folklore for six centuries, and still spoken of as a living memory during the Civil War of the 17th century, when the last of the Norman-founded castles passed out of use as military establishments.

The huge keep of Colchester Castle – similar in plan to the Tower of London – was probably built by Gundulf, Bishop of Rochester, in about 1083. It is a self-contained and formidable defensive structure with massive walls, 12 ft (3.7 m) thick, broadening to 17½ ft (5 m) at the plinth. Bricks from the Roman temple of Claudius, on the site of which the keep was built, were reused in its construction.

In 1070, just a few years after the Battle of Hastings, the motte and bailey of Carisbrooke Castle, on the Isle of Wight, were built. This is one of the earliest Norman castles. The first post-Conquest castles tended to be of earthwork and timber construction, and were rebuilt later in stone. About 1,000 motte-and-bailey forts are thought to have been built in Britain.

ABOVE: *Launceston Castle, in Cornwall, is another very early Norman castle, whose keep – like those at Colchester and the Tower of London – was originally built in stone rather than wood. A wooden structure's great vulnerability to fire meant that stone was vastly preferable, as long as materials, time and labour were available.*

RIGHT: *William I ordered the construction of Lincoln Castle in 1068. His engineers utilized the remains of the Roman walls, which enclosed the outer bailey of the castle, while a lower Roman enclosure farther down became the medieval city. Lincoln quickly became, and remained, a castle-town of great importance.*

Even so, it is doubtful that such a vast and perilous enterprise as the Norman conquest of England could have been carried through to success without the inspiration and energy of William I, a general and military administrator of the first rank. William was noted for many things, but not least for his skill as a builder. His religious fervour, like that of his race – so prodigal in the building of churches, cathedrals and abbeys – undoubtedly assisted his success as a military architect; indeed, clerical designers and craftsmen assisted him and his sons at all stages of their castle programme.

Ordericus Vitalis, one of the best of the early chroniclers, insists that the Saxons were defeated and conquered because they had not adopted the castle. As we have seen, under Edward the Confessor the castle, in so far as it existed at all in England, was an alien import remaining in largely alien hands. However, the failure of the English to maintain modern fixed defences was only one side of the story. Equally important was the speed with which William provided himself with them. He came fully prepared. The chronicler Wace, writing a hundred years later but doubtless using lost sources, says that William brought over the materials for a prefabricated fort: that

is, wooden sections already cut and drilled, together with the fittings. Wace says that the fort was erected immediately after the landing at Pevensey, and was complete by the end of the day. Thus William moved to Hastings from a fortified base, very likely a ditch and palisade, with a powerful gateway. Ordericus Vitalis says it had 'a very strong rampart'. Nor was this all. Immediately after his victory at Hastings, William consolidated his position by building a castle there. The work is portrayed in the Bayeux Tapestry. After this, his first move was to Dover. There he found a rudimentary castle, built perhaps in the Norman fashion. But he was not satisfied, and spent eight days rebuilding and strengthening it. Then he went to Canterbury, and 'built a tower' (presumably of wood, with a defensive ditch). Before arranging the surrender of London, he crossed the Thames at Wallingford, where he deposited experts to start work on another castle. So, like the methodical Romans before him, William moved forward at each stage only when he had a prepared defence to fall back on. Later, after the formal surrender of the English clergy and nobility, and his coronation at Westminster, William had the country surveyed, and he immediately ordered a vast programme of

(continued on page 47)

THE TOWER OF LONDON

LOCATION

The Tower of London stands on the north bank of the Thames, near Tower Bridge, in central London.

HISTORICAL IMPORTANCE

By 1066, when the Saxon monarchy was in its final months, London was a thriving commercial and trading centre, and had become the largest town in Britain. At dusk on 14 October that year, King Harold was killed on the battlefield of Hastings, and Duke William of Normandy set about securing his victory. He began a circuitous advance on London, his army laying the countryside to waste, and, after receiving the submission of the English leaders and the citizens of London, he entered the city and was crowned king of England on Christmas Day. The Tower was one of three castles – powerful and intimidating symbols of the new order – that William built in London. Successive monarchs added to it so that, by the 13th century, it had become one of the strongest and best-defended fortresses in the country.

NOTABLE FEATURES

The Tower became known as the White Tower during the reign of Henry III, who ordered its walls to be whitewashed. This emphasized its scale and heightened its impact. Henry also initiated a huge and costly construction programme, building residential and administrative quarters and raising the first of the curtain walls, set with 13 flanking towers. His son, Edward I, expanded the fortress's area, building the outer curtain wall, with its six towers, and excavating a new and broader moat, which remained filled with water until the 19th century. In the course of its 900-year history, the Tower of London has fulfilled a number of functions, including that of royal palace, mint, prison and armoury. Today it still houses the Crown Jewels.

castle building. It may be that William's early English castles were simply ditch-and-rampart palisades, with a central wooden tower built on a natural prominence or low man-made mound. Then, when more time was available, the mottes became more ambitious.

Essentially, the Norman castle was a fortified post from which a small body of armoured cavalry could range over an occupied area, and to which they retired if attacked by a superior force. It contained a hall, usually on the first storey of a wooden building, for security purposes, with offices below; a well; a kitchen; sleeping-quarters for the men and horses; storerooms and workshops and, as a rule, a chapel. All of this area was surrounded by a ditch outside a bank. The entrance was by a bridge across the ditch, to a gap in the bank, further strengthened by a high timber fence. The whole defensive area formed the bailey. In time a wooden watchtower was added to overlook the bailey. Towards the end of the 11th century these watchtowers became more elaborate, and were placed on mounds of increasing height. Then the motte-top developed its own fence and gate, and was reached by a flying bridge, or a gangway, itself protected by a timber palisade. So we soon have a castle (or keep, or donjon) within a castle.

Timber motte-and-bailey castles were cheap and quick to construct. But they were temporary. When timber is in contact with earth it soon rots. The next stage, therefore, was to follow the Roman custom of raising timber buildings on stone sleeper-walls. The third stage came when the keep was entirely rebuilt in stone. No Norman king or lord built in timber if there was time, labour and material to build in stone: for the great destroyer of early castles was fire, and a stone keep could be made virtually fireproof.

That is why the keep was always the first part of the castle to be rebuilt in stone. The lord then had privacy and safety, and a secure place to keep his documents, money and prisoners. There were usually three or four rooms, stacked vertically, with smaller rooms built into the thickness of his walls. Since everything had to go in and out through the same entrance in the keep, a form of lobby or landing (called the forebuilding) was soon added, and the upper floor of this often formed the chapel. The roof was a weak point. It was built first of thatch, later of wooden shingles (usually of oak), clay tiles, stone slates, and lead. But thatch and shingles could be fired; and heavy missiles could crash through tiles and slates. So walls were carried up above the roofs, to protect them from siege engines, and the resulting parapet provided with a wall walk, so becoming a fighting platform and developing into battlements. But the arcs of fire from the battlements did not cover the base of the wall and, to deal with the problem, wooden galleries, holding archers and missiles, were hung out of the walls on brackets.

In the years immediately after the Battle of Hastings, William's aim was to put up as many of these small castles as he could conveniently

The rectangular stone tower of Castle Rising, built probably in about 1138, lies within the earthwork ramparts of a bailey, itself part of an extensive series of banks and ditches covering some 12 acres (5 ha). The remains of the keep's fine living quarters reflect its builder's status – William de Albini, Earl of Lincoln, had married Henry I's widow.

defend; and his tenants-in-chief and officials fanned out all over England and its borders in compliance with his instructions. During this first phase, castles (usually of wood) were set up overlooking towns, on the highest ground available, and often adjoining a river.

Not all these earliest castles had mottes, which were only gradually, during William's time, coming to be accepted as an indispensable part of a standard castle. Obviously, construction of mottes varied enormously according to local earth and rock conditions. A natural rock (which made undermining virtually impossible), with water available, was the ideal mound. Building an artificial motte was much more complicated than just throwing up earth, which could not provide a stable foundation for timber, let alone stone. It had to be levelled up with reinforcing layers of rock, or hard-beaten earth, or covered with an outer crust of clay. Heavy superstructures set up on a poorly made motte soon began to lean outwards, and were a death-trap under siege. The ditches had to be carefully worked too. The simplest were v-shaped. But wet moats were obviously desirable for a variety of reasons. Throughout the Middle Ages the strongest castles nearly always had water defences – and this was a more serious problem of earth-moving engineering, entailing the controlled diversion of streams and rivers. Even with dry ditches, the bank might well have timber faces, to bind the earth together.

Once the Normans had time to set up their castles in stone, their tremendous sense of beauty and quality, so powerfully expressed in Durham Cathedral, asserted itself, and the outer faces, at least, were made if possible of ashlar, that is, wrought smooth stone. Behind these ashlar blocks a core of rubble, bound with mortar, was rammed home, while wood ties framed and bound the wall until the mortar had set. Sometimes, the entire wall was of mortared rubble, which set within wooden shutters. The Normans were already developing powerful engines for siege warfare, and such towers could be adapted for castle building, though they also used high cranes. (Medieval crane wheels can still be seen in the towers of the walls at Canterbury, and at Salisbury and Peterborough cathedrals.) When the walls were finished they were, if possible, coated with plaster and whitewashed – a practice reflected in the names of the White Tower in London, and the White Castle of the Welsh borders. Some of the earliest stone castles in England had primitive lead plumbing; and even glass has been found at Ascot d'Oyly and Deddington, though these were 12th-century castles.

William's castle-building programme was continued remorselessly by his successors, Rufus and Henry I. Thus the closing decades of the 11th century and the long reign of Henry I were marked by continuous castle building, increasingly in stone rather than wood, under royal direction. The rectangular stone keep, which dominated major castle building in this period, was not exactly new, as we have seen. But it became a peculiarly Norman-Angevin institution. Keeps were characterized by exceptionally thick walls, and wide, low-projecting buttresses. Sometimes they were set on a particularly firm mound, more often on the hard ground of the bailey. They were two to four storeys high, and divided internally by a partition wall. The entrance was on the second storey, reached by external stairs, later

ABOVE: *At the end of the 11th century, Roger de Poitou built an enormous stone keep at Lancaster, in Cumbria. The design was typical of Norman keeps, with exceptionally thick walls and wide, low-projecting buttresses. The keep now forms part of HM Prison Lancaster Castle.*

RIGHT: *Durham Castle, above the River Wear, originated as a fortified residence that was built for the bishop of Durham in 1072. For the privilege of exerting supreme control over his territory – the palatinate – the bishop was obliged to supply an army in the event of any invasion from the north.*

covered and protected by the forebuilding. The principal hall was on the second or third storey, often with an internal mural gallery, and with mural chambers opening off it. There were fireplaces, one (sometimes two) chapels, very deep walls (sometimes with lead pipes carrying the water up two or three storeys), and straight or spiral staircases, often in the thickness of the wall. These square keeps were sometimes, in effect, gatehouses. More often, however, they were inside a stone bailey wall.

These great square stone towers continued to be built in England throughout the 12th century. As the century progressed, refinements were added: portcullises, machicolations in the entrance passages, *meurtrières* and arrow-loops. These defensive devices were built into the structure as the mechanics of siege warfare improved. There was an unremitting technological battle between the two sides. Men were aware that the great stone keep, however strong, was not the perfect answer to enormous siege engines and miners. The weakness lay in the corners, which could be prised open by men with crowbars working under cover. Some military engineers believed in the alternative of the shell keep; that is, replacing the wooden palisades round the top of the motte by a strong stone wall, with the castle

buildings ranged alongside it within. Then, in addition, the palisades of the bailey were converted into walls, with stone towers built at intervals to overlook the entire face of the curtain. These walls could be equipped with movable bridges, linking the various sections, but isolating them too if a particular section fell to assault. The general layout of such castles offered better protection against high-trajectory stone-throwing engines, like the pivotal-beam *trebouchet*, or the fixed-stop mangonel. They were also equipped with a massive gateway, usually the first part of the outer curtain wall to be converted to stone, with its own defensive barbican outside the castle perimeter. A shell-keep castle with a towered curtain wall placed less reliance on a single defensive feature than the tower-keep. It gave the defenders much more mobility within their perimeter, faced the attackers with a greater variety of problems (and hazards), and meant that the fight could go on even after they had won substantial successes.

Yet though one can produce a typology of castles, Roman-style uniformity was lacking. No two were alike. Topographical features, the taste or ingenuity of individual lords, availability of money, materials and labour combined to make each castle unique, once the primitive motte-and-bailey stage was over.

(continued on page 52)

EDINBURGH CASTLE

LOCATION

Edinburgh Castle is located in the centre of Edinburgh, at the western end of High Street.

HISTORICAL IMPORTANCE

The name 'Edinburgh' is derived from that of Edwin, king of Northumbria. In the 7th century, he built a wooden fortress on the once-volcanic outcrop of rock that towers 300 ft (90 m) above the modern city. Commanding wide views over the Firth of Forth, this secure vantage point became the site of a great stone citadel. The history of Edinburgh Castle is intricately bound up with Scotland's national history. The castle came under siege many times during the Middle Ages. In 1296 it was captured by Edward I of England and retaken by the nephew of Robert the Bruce 17 years later. It was also the birthplace of James VI of Scotland, who after the death of Elizabeth I, acceded to the throne of England as James I.

Oliver Cromwell besieged the castle in 1650 and, after its surrender, used the fortress as a headquarters for his occupying army. The castle has served as a royal palace, a prison, a treasury and as the storehouse for Scotland's records.

NOTABLE FEATURES

The citadel within the curtain wall that surrounds the summit of the rock contains several buildings. Although many of these date from the Napoleonic period, some remains of the medieval castle survive. One of the oldest buildings is a small, early 12th-century chapel dedicated to St Margaret, wife of Malcolm III, who died in 1093, and who was later canonized. The remains of another early building – an L-shaped tower constructed by David II in the late 13th century – are also visible. The vestiges of a vaulted chamber lie in the Half-Moon Battery, built in the late 16th century. In the late 19th century, the Gatehouse was rebuilt and the Great Hall restored.

The need for decoration within a castle must have been all the stronger when we consider that it was the home of a rich man, the only one he had, unlike the church, which he merely visited. There was a compulsion to make it more comfortable and beautiful, not least to express the ego of an ambitious man (and his wife) who had carved out an estate for himself in a hostile country. Even as the great stone keeps were rising, a conflict began to develop between comfort and security. But then the keep itself, the great military innovation of the 11th century, was a dangerously inflexible concept. The idea of combining all the main accommodation and services in one building necessarily produced uncomfortable living conditions. The demands of social architecture and military engineering were often incompatible, or mutually antagonistic, and so produced compromises in which both suffered. Square or rectangular shapes produce blind space at the points of greatest vulnerability. So a polygonal or round shape was safer. But the need to stack rooms produced difficulties in either case. Unless expensively built of vaulted stone, floors involved timber, which exposed the building to fire and collapse. Staircases built into the wall necessarily weakened it. Recesses for chimneys, fireplaces, sanitation and storage had to be hollowed out at the expense of the strength and stability of the main wall; window-openings, to admit light and air, were absolute weaknesses. They performed no military function. The designers replaced windows with small slits at the bottom of the main walls. But neither these, nor the windows, were of any use to defending archers. And all these openings and recesses were the first targets for the siege engineers, seeking to begin the process of reducing the keep to rubble.

Then again the entrance caused endless and often insoluble troubles. It was the weakest point of all. So the strongest castle had only one entrance, and only one door in the keep. And since even the single entrance was at risk, it had to have extra defences. These, by their very nature, increased the bottleneck. A strong keep always had a good keep well: at Windsor it was lined with dressed stone to a depth of over 60 ft (18 m) below ground. But apart from water, everything else, and everybody, had to come and go through one door. Even with a forebuilding to produce a landing, life could become intolerable. Most, perhaps all, of a castle's existence was spent in peacetime conditions, and the temptation to make life more comfortable at the expense of structural security often proved irresistible. Even under siege conditions, the keep-castle was not as formidable as it looked. The small force it could accommodate was no threat to an army – merely to the surrounding peasants. It might be impregnable, but it was also a trap. However massive, it could hold only a limited number of people for a limited time; and a relatively small detachment from an enemy army could lock them inside, until disease, starvation and plummeting morale compelled surrender. The future lay with a rather different type of castle, as we shall see.

(continued on page 57)

Fortifications at Alnwick, in Northumberland, began in the 1090s. By 1150, a stone shell keep and curtain walls had been built. In 1172, and again in 1174, it was besieged by William the Lion, King of Scotland. In the second siege, William was captured, hastening the end of a rebellion that had challenged Henry II's authority.

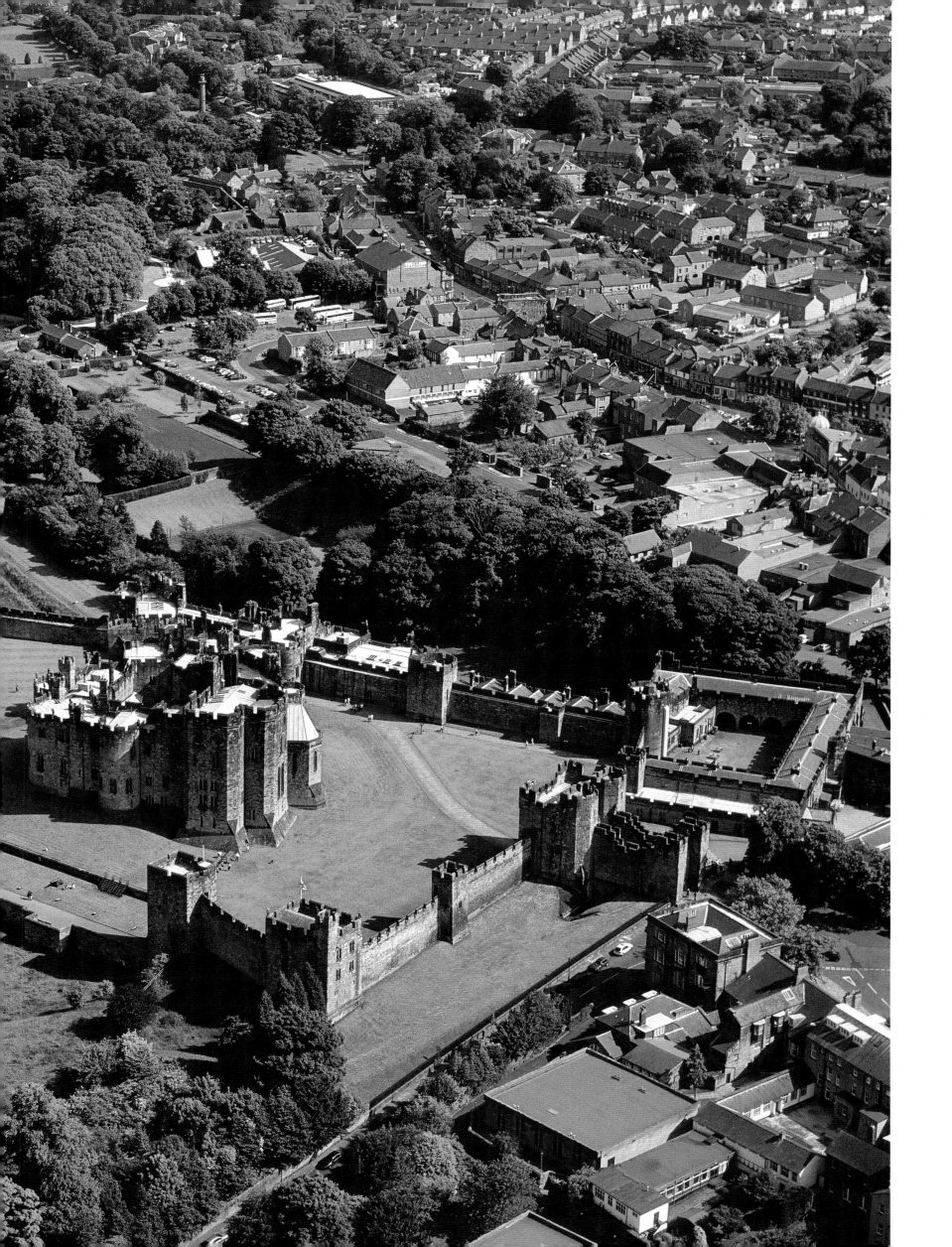

The Norman castle also posed a social and political problem. As we have seen, William I could not have conquered and held England without building castles in large numbers, and entrusting his tenants-in-chief with their custody. Many more came into existence as his successors pushed into Wales and to the north. At one time there may have been as many as 1,000 motte-and-bailey castles. But this dispersal of power to feudatories necessarily posed a threat to the monarchy. William the Conqueror was well aware of this. He increased his own power correspondingly, both in England and Normandy; in fact in the duchy of Normandy his conquest of England gave him sufficient authority and means to enforce the rule that no castle might be built without his consent. This power of the duke over private castles is the earliest case we have of interference in the customary rights of a Norman vassal. William seems to have established the right, formalized in the duchy customs in 1091, shortly after his death, to occupy any castle at will; and he undoubtedly exercised it in his last years, when many baronial castles were garrisoned by his troops.

In England William modified the feudal system to check baronial autonomy. He combined several thousand small estates into fewer than 200 major lordships, held by tenants-in-chief. The lands forming a lord's endowment were known collectively as his 'honour' (i.e. 'that which give a man distinction'). The lord's chief residence, his castle, was the head of the honour and its administrative and business centre. The contemporary term for a district with which the distribution of land had been planned for the maintenance of a particular fortress was *castellaria*. Such a consolidation of estates around castles enabled a small occupying force of Normans to hold down a nation. From William's point of view a few large barons were easier to control than a multitude of small ones. Moreover, he established the point, maintained in theory at least until the days of Charles I, that the monarchy might occupy at will any castle or house of a tenant-in-chief. He had a further institutional device to hold his great men in check. The knight's fee, the basic unit of military tenure in post-Conquest England, was a Norman institution. In England William was able to implant it from scratch, and completely subject it to his authority and purpose. The knight-service he accordingly imposed on his English tenants-in-chief was so heavy that few of them could afford to enfief knights much in excess of what they owed the duke. Whereas in Normandy the size of a lord's military retinue bore no relation to the knight-service he had to provide, in England virtually all the baronial knights could be 'called up' by the king at the least threat of trouble.

The system worked, albeit with some outbreaks of trouble, well enough under the Conqueror and his two strong-minded sons, Rufus

and Henry Beauclerk. But any medieval monarchy, however strong, was vulnerable to a failure of male heirs. William and his sons permitted the construction of private wooden castles in some quantity. Major works, especially of stone, were either royal, or held by tenants-in-chief under stringent safeguards. Then came the disaster of the *White Ship* in 1120, which drowned Beauclerk's only son; and it is significant that, after this mishap, which foreshadowed a disputed succession, we first hear of major castle works by individual subjects.

With Henry's death in 1135 and the subsequent struggle between Matilda and Stephen of Blois, the great age of the 'adulterine castle' opened. The Anglo-Saxon Chronicle recorded: 'and they filled the whole land with these castles. They sorely burdened the unhappy people of the country with forced labour on the castles. And when the castles were made they filled them with devils and wicked men.' Many of the adulterines had very short lives. Some were very small indeed, and have vanished virtually without trace. At the time they constantly changed hands. There was also a great crop of counter-castles or siege-castles, set up either to assault or cancel out existing structures – at, for example, Dunster, Ludlow, Corfe and Arundel.

Not all the castles built during the anarchy were small and ephemeral. Moreover, many important existing castles, including royal fortresses, fell into baronial hands. Nevertheless, the memory of the first three Norman kings was so potent that even during the anarchy at least some great lords sought to introduce elements of legality into the ownership and use of castles. Major tenants-in-chief always tried to obtain a legal basis for their actions, and their tenure of castles. And there is evidence that the greater barons were tiring of their mutual struggle. By the mid-12th century, it was guessed, there were some 1,115 unlicensed castles. Incessant castle warfare posed grave problems to big landowners. Contemporary siege techniques were not equal to the easy reduction even of small castles. If a surprise assault failed, the attacker settled down to starving out the garrison, meanwhile living off the neighbouring countryside. Forced to abandon the siege, they destroyed the remaining crops and food supplies, to deny them to the defenders. Even when there was no actual fighting the depredations of the 'castlemen' were intolerable. The barons might not care much about the sufferings of their peasants, but they hated to see their own revenues fall. Moreover, the greater lords found that their own vassals, by building castles which could stand up to anything short of a regular siege, were becoming uncontrollable. Hence the big men began to make private peace treaties among themselves, regulating areas where the royal writ no longer ran. One of their chief aims was to prevent the building of private castles, and reduce the number of existing ones – an aim traditionally associated with royal policy. The growing desire for peace found expression in the Treaty of Winchester, signed in 1153, which composed the differences between Stephen and Matilda's son, the future Henry II, and opened the way for the peaceful accession of the first Angevin ruler. It contained special provision for the castles of London, Windsor, Oxford, Lincoln and Winchester. Stephen's reign marked the apogee of the private castle in England; the coming of Henry II not only brought the problem under control for 250 years, but also introduced a new epoch into military architecture.

PLANTAGENET CASTLES

Henry II was the ideal sovereign to end a period of anarchy dominated by unlicensed private castles. He held strongly to the view that the powerful and properly controlled royal castle was the very foundation of civil law, and that private castles, except in the supervised possession of men absolutely loyal to the crown, were the enemies of order.

Henry II inherited his father's literacy, expertise and passionate regard for the rule of law. And he founded in England a great line of builder-kings: Richard, John, Henry III, Edward I and Edward III; only two of his progeny, Edward II and Richard II, failed to become outstanding builders of castles and, perhaps in consequence, both were murdered in castle dungeons. Henry II's first problem, however, when he assumed control in England, was not to build but to destroy. Estimates of the number of castles he smashed to bits range from 375 to 1,115 (the latter is certainly too high, since it represents the total of unlicensed castles). He was not a great general, but his defensive campaigns and his anti-baronial police actions were dashing, original and almost entirely successful. His ability to take even the strongest castles was famous. As a rule he did it by a lightning raid without warning, a rapid investment, then a massive and shattering assault. By such means he seized a number of castles hitherto regarded as impregnable. This had important social consequences. In the 1130s and 1140s the balance of advantage had swung towards the defence and, as a consequence of castle building, legitimate authority had become divorced from actual power. A handful of men in a strong castle could defy an army. Henry II reversed the trend not merely by his huge siege train and engines, improving on his father's ideas, but by the specialized force of mercenaries he formed for internal policing. These routiers, mainly from Flanders, were long-service foot-soldiers, fed and clothed by Henry, who had them specially trained and equipped for ruthless siege operations.

Thus Henry was able to take by force any powerful stone castle that defied him. Happily, in England his reputation preceded him. His first act was to command all baronial occupiers to relinquish royal castles in their custody. What Henry was doing was to enforce to the letter the right the king had always claimed to occupy and control any fortification beyond a certain size. At the beginning of his reign private castles outnumbered royal castles by five to one. Within ten years most non-royal castles had been confiscated and destroyed or placed in reliable hands. The king did not forbid private castle building completely. Faithful supporters were allowed, very occasionally, to build new castles, or expand and improve old ones. Thus Berkeley Castle was refashioned, and provided with one of the first turreted curtain walls in England. Henry also carried through an immense programme of royal castle building and the systematic modernization of existing fortresses. In some cases, refortification of

(continued on page 62)

The Norman advance into southwestern Wales was marked by a spate of castle building. One of the earliest, and largest, was Pembroke, begun in the 1090s. It was followed in about 1100 by the first defences at Carew, seen here from the air, some 5 miles (8 km) away, built by Gerald de Windsor, former constable of Pembroke.

PEMBROKE CASTLE

LOCATION

*Pembroke Castle is located in Pembroke town centre,
at the west end of Main Street.*

HISTORICAL IMPORTANCE

Predating the remarkable series of fortresses that Edward I built in
Wales to subdue the Welsh, Pembroke Castle was one of the
greatest castles in Britain. The first castle on the site − a rocky
promontory overlooking the river − was an earthwork
fortification built in 1093 by Arnulph, a Norman who was the
son of Roger de Montgomery, one of William I's oldest friends.
In about 1200, King John granted the castle, then part of the
great marcher lordship of Pembroke, to William Marshall.
Although he was originally a landless younger son, Marshall rose
to become one of the most powerful men in the kingdom, acting
as regent during the minority of John's heir, the young Henry III.
Known thereafter by his title of Earl of Pembroke, Marshall
benefited greatly from the lordship of Pembroke, which brought
him power and wealth. The land included rich arable acreage, and
was ideally situated as a base for military expeditions to Ireland.
The birthplace of the future Henry VII in 1456, Pembroke Castle
was to remain almost unchallenged until the Civil War, when it
was besieged and slighted by Oliver Cromwell in 1648.

NOTABLE FEATURES

William Marshall, Earl of Pembroke, was responsible for the first
stone construction on the site. This comprised the enormous
round tower, with walls almost 20 ft (6 m) at the base, and the
wall of the inner bailey. Some 50 years later, a second curtain wall,
set with flanking towers, was built, greatly adding to the area of
the castle. A gatehouse and a barbican, with all the most up-to-
date defensive devices, were also added. In parts of the outer
curtain on the south side, the wall was built to double thickness.

royal castles was accompanied by building of town walls, forming large defended areas in which the castle served as a keep. Henry was an innovator in military architecture. At Orford, he moved away from the rectangular keep, with its blind and vulnerable corners, towards the circular or polygonal keep. Orford was habitable by 1168, and two years later it had a new-style curtain wall with rectangular towers, now alas vanished.

At the same time Henry did not discard the rectangular keep. At Dover, a vast building programme was carried out throughout the 1180s. This included a big cubical keep, a curtain wall with 14 square towers, and two powerful gatehouses. Dover incorporated a number of other innovations, such as immensely strong mural towers, powerful gateways and the emergence of the new principle of concentricity – which was to dominate castle building throughout the 13th and 14th centuries. Mural towers, especially if they projected, prevented mining since they covered every foot of the wall. Once a strong enceinte was put up, the keep became less important. Square or rectangular keeps were easier to build; and, from a domestic viewpoint, more convenient.

Both Henry II's regal sons, Richard and John, were tremendous castle builders. Until well into the 13th century, the Holy Land continued to be the main testing-ground and inspiration for new ideas in fortifications and siege techniques. Richard brought back from the Third Crusade not only new military concepts but artillery engineers and builders of *arbalistae*. By his day the accurate use of stone-throwing engines and mining techniques had been brought to the point where the existence beneath the walls of a single dead angle, or any place that could not be reached by missiles hurled by the defenders, imperilled the whole fortress.

John, too, spent large sums of money modernizing his castles and building new ones, though little of his work has survived. John left his infant son Henry III about 60 castles, some of which were becoming obsolete, plus a large group of palaces and manor houses. Henry's guardian, Hubert de Burgh, a leading expert on castles, took the work in hand, and throughout Henry's minority substantial sums were spent on repairs and improvements. Once he was of age, Henry continued the policy. He also began to build even more vigorously than his mentor, though his greatest work, Westminster Abbey, lies outside our scope. In the military sphere, his masterpiece is Kenilworth, in Warwickshire. That was a Norman foundation, and Henry II, John and Henry III all spent large sums on modernizing it. But it was Henry III who turned it into the strongest fortress in the Midlands, with the exception perhaps of Nottingham. He seems to have possessed quite a sense of military strategy, seen later in his son Edward I. He recognized that unless a castle was built on a high, spectacular rock, the surest form of defence was water – not a narrow moat or even a river, but acres and acres of deep water. It was Henry and his experts who created the great lake at Kenilworth, by damming a series of streams that flow through the valley, and they erected two more lines of moats on the north side – the only side not protected by the lake-water. The water fortifications covered over 100 acres (40 ha), bigger by far than a similar scheme at Caerphilly (*see*

page 102). Water defences on this scale had to be kept in constant and expensive repair, but they had the inestimable advantage that the huge siege engines, which dominated siege warfare from the age of Henry II to the coming of large cannon, could not be easily, if at all, brought within range of the curtain walls, let alone the keep.

During periods of peace, the medieval mind having an incurable objection to looking far ahead, castles fell swiftly into decay. Maintenance was a constant struggle against the ravages of storm damage, for a good castle was nearly always in an exposed spot; the results of poor workmanship were another perennial problem, for most castles were built in haste, with forced labour. So tower and walls cracked and fell, and roofs were stripped of lead by high winds. Money was always short but, if essential repairs were not done swiftly, the damage quickly became irreparable. The royal system of authorizing work, however, was slow.

Of course, we cannot understand the medieval castle as an institution unless we appreciate its economic as well as its military functions. It did not stand in isolation but as part of a system, inseparable from its dependent area. A *castellaria* and *chatellenie* comprised castle, lands, feudal duties and fiscal arrangements – normally very complicated ones if the castle was royal. Often, monopolies of mills, ovens and other basic services were created primarily to maintain castles; in fact the erection of a fortress made the creation of monopolies inevitable. This was one reason why castles were unpopular with the peasants. Townsmen might have a different attitude, especially in the 'new towns'. Created in increasing numbers from the time of Rufus onwards (Carlisle was the first), here merchants, shopkeepers and artisans were attracted by privileges and fiscal concessions. But they were milked too, to keep the walls in repair. The possession of a stronghold without its 'natural' sources of revenue was abhorrent to the medieval mind; normally they expected it to make a profit.

Inevitably, the flaw in the argument was that, in the long run, he who held the castles exploited the neighbourhood. A castle could not function for long without its locality, or vice-versa. Castle-guard was a regular form of military service. There was also the duty to work on buildings and earthworks. The peasant might not like neighbouring castles, but little towns tended to spring up in their shadows for protection, and their inhabitants were often responsible for keeping the walls upright and in repair.

In peacetime, townsmen were allowed to cultivate strips right up to the castle walls or the edge of the moat. But when war came the ditches had to be cleaned out ruthlessly, and the lean-to's that had accumulated against the walls pulled down. These townlets were the first to suffer if a castle were regularly invested. Indeed all the neighbourhood suffered. The besiegers first wasted the land before concentrating on the castle. The usual expectation was that this would do the trick and compel surrender without a fight. No one enjoyed a siege, which was slow and hideously costly in terms of lives, money and property. If a castle were well stocked and in good repair, with a loyal constable and a garrison in good heart, the odds were that the besiegers would simply go away.

The ruined curtain wall of Conisburgh Castle, near Doncaster, in South Yorkshire, contains a remarkable keep. Of a design unknown anywhere else in Britain, it was built in about 1180 by Hamelin, Henry II's half-brother. Essentially a circular building, the keep has six enormous angular buttresses spaced at equal intervals around it. One of the buttresses contains a chapel.

But if everyone tried to avoid sieges, sometimes they were inescapable. Siege warfare was, increasingly, a matter for experts. John, for instance, had a corps of engineers, or *ingeniatores*, a member of which was sometimes styled a *balistarius*, though strictly speaking this meant a crossbowman who used a *balista*. The crossbowmen were the elite of the garrison. The weapon came into general use in the early 12th century, although the English were unusual in preferring the longbow; it had a much higher rate of fire – five to one – and the great advantage that the bowman could keep his eyes on the enemy while reloading. But even the English admitted that the crossbow was a superior weapon in siege warfare, especially in defence. The first true arrow-slits for crossbows began to appear just before 1190, in the multi-storey fighting gallery of the Avranches Tower at Dover, and at Framlingham in Suffolk. Thereafter, crossbowmen rapidly emerged as a specialist class of professional soldiers.

In the 15th century, the crossbow's range grew to 370–380 yards (340–350 m). It was designed primarily to force besieging men and machines to keep their distance. (The besieging bowmen had wood screens, called mantlets, to protect themselves.) The earliest machines were wheeled battering rams, with iron heads, on the Roman model; but these were already obsolescent by the late 12th century. Far more

useful, in practice, were various forms of penthouse, or cats, used to protect men throwing brushwood to make causeways across ditches, undermining, or piling combustibles against wooden sections of the walls. Artillery included the *petriaria*, which hurled huge rocks, catapults or scorpions for smaller stones, or the medium-sized *ballista* or mangonel which threw stones weighing about half a hundredweight (25 kg). By the end of the 12th century some projectile engines were as powerful as early cannon. Stones were specially quarried for the bigger engines. When they ran out, paving stones and millstones were hurled, as well as iron bars, darts and sharpened poles. Other missiles included pots of quicklime or burning pitch, and flaming torches. But stories of boiling oil and molten lead are probably fictitious; both were too expensive. Fire was what the defenders feared most, for even supposedly fireproof castles were crammed with combustible materials. Next came mining: that is, digging tunnels with wooden supports, which were afterwards fired, causing subsidence. With gunpowder came the true mine.

A strong, well-defended castle usually fell, if it fell at all, to a combination of weapons and privation. Against a well-defended castle persistence was the supreme virtue. An up-to-date castle rarely yielded to direct assault, unless it was unexpected.

(continued on page 69)

ABOVE: *Henry II was famed for his ability to take and destroy castles, but he was also a great castle builder. The keep of Orford Castle in Suffolk, which he built in the 1160s, shows the development in military architecture, which was moving away from the rectangular structure, with its blind and vulnerable corners, towards the circular or polygonal tower.*

RIGHT: *Framlingham Castle, in Suffolk, was built by the powerful Bigod family on a well-defended site, probably in the 1190s. The castle has no central keep, and takes the form of an enclosure defended by a curtain wall set with 12 rectangular flanking towers. The hall of an earlier castle, which was destroyed by Henry II, was built into the curtain wall.*

With the intensification of castle technology, there was an insatiable demand for expert craftsmen, who were increasingly well paid and therefore figure more prominently in the records. In the accounts, these men are all termed engineers, a name deriving from their skill in designing, making, dismantling and transporting siege engines, and directing operations from them. They were, in fact, soldiers, but they could build castles and churches, too – in fact they turned their hand to anything involving mechanical ingenuity.

From the early 13th century many royal craftsmen begin to figure by name in the accounts, and there is a growing tendency to specialize. Most siege engineers were carpenters by training, and it is carpenters who figure most prominently in the records. But there was also the *petrarius*, mason or stonecutter; the *quareator*, or quarryman; the *mier* or *cementarius*, the stone-mason; *fossatores*, who worked on moats and dry ditches; and the miners who were responsible for the vaults and rockwork of castles. The *hurdatores* made the 'hoardings' or projecting wooden archer-galleries. *Piccatores* were employed in demolishing hostile fortifications. The engineers were the highest paid. This group of highly skilled specialists were directly attached to the king, sometimes moving about with him, sometimes detached for supervisory duties at a group of castles. They were precursors of the royal engineers. Mason-architects were also multi-skilled.

The emergence of skilled craftsmen, equally adept at creating within a domestic as well as a military context, inevitably reinforced the tendency for castles to acquire more comfort than was safe. The rot set in at the big royal palaces, like Westminster, Woodstock and Clarendon, where there were few concessions to military needs, and where the latest architectural refinements were introduced. Henry III, who loved comfort and beauty, set the pace. From his father John, a great builder of manor houses and hunting-boxes, he inherited a score or more, prototypes of the fortified manor houses of the later Middle Ages. They usually had a moat, some kind of defensive tower, and a palisade. Such houses Henry loved to adorn and modernize, thus bringing luxurious habits deep into the countryside, to the scorn or envy of austere castelans.

Palaces and manor houses, even if fortified, were insecure, partly because they made generous use of wood. For castles as such, wood was rapidly going out of use under Henry. But if wood was disappearing from the externals of castles, Henry III was busy bringing it into the interior, in the form of wainscoting for the chief rooms. It is not easy to visualize what these 13th-century castles were like inside, since they are now either bare and ruinous, or submerged in later work. Domestic accommodation was more often rebuilt than

were the defences, so few early halls have survived. These walls were usually whitewashed, with the line of the stones picked out in red; and, from the mid-12th century, adorned with paintings. Medieval man was desperate for colour and lightness, especially in castles where windows were small. So it is a mistake for restorers to show bare stone internally. External whitewashing was the rule, too. Internally, the walls were sometimes plastered as well. Henry III's favourite decorative motif, in both his castles and his palaces, was gold stars on a green background. He had elaborate paintings in his castle-chamber at Winchester. Even humble castles might be elaborately decorated too, with riotous colour and masses of gold paint.

From the 13th century on we are able to gather innumerable details about other aspects of castle life in England. King John ordered new kitchens to be built at Marlborough and Ludgershall, capable of roasting two or three oxen in each. Fireplaces had first made their appearance in the late 11th century and by the 14th century they had become elaborate affairs.

So the quest for comfort continued. More staircases were added and decorative windows made their appearance. Soon they were filled with glass. Many castles also had internal windows, peepholes called squints. They usually looked down from the solar or great chamber to the hall, to allow the lord or king to know what was going on there; or to the chapel, so that mass could be heard and seen without getting out of bed.

Sanitary arrangements were also becoming more elaborate. Medieval manners placed much emphasis on cleanliness of the hands. People washed their hands on entering the hall for meals (or on leaving). So lavers, the secular version of the church piscina, were usually to be found near its entrance. For bathing the usual practice was simply to fill casks or barrels with water. But, according to a description of Edward II's canopied bath, which was set into a tiled floor, bathing arrangements were becoming more elaborate.

Certainly, the lavatories (privies, or garderobes, as they were called) were much better than one might have expected. Most big castle chambers had a fireplace and a privy each. Where practicable, the privy was placed as far away as possible, on account of the smell, at the end of a passage in the thickness of the wall. Where the wall was not thick enough, the privy was corbelled out, like an external buttress. Shoots were built for the discharge, sometimes barred, concealed by masonry screens or protected by grotesque masks.

Smells of a different kind tended to infest all parts of a castle, especially the hall or refectory, unless it was 'strewed' often enough with sweet-smelling herbs. Henry III provided mats for the first time, but only in his chapels, not in his halls; and Matthew Paris says the Londoners were shocked when they heard that Eleanor of Castile, bringing wasteful Spanish fashions in her train, actually put carpets on the floor of her bedroom.

Despite everything, castles were still very uncomfortable (and deathly cold) places at the end of the reign of the fastidious Henry III. It was left to his son, the brilliant Lord Edward, to introduce a completely new epoch in castle building, which greatly improved their comforts as well as revolutionized their military structure.

PREVIOUS PAGES: *The medieval historian Matthew Paris described Dover Castle as 'the key of England'. It is set on a hilltop overlooking the English Channel at its narrowest point, and its earliest stone defences – the enormously strong keep, the inner curtain wall and a large section of the outer curtain – are the work of Henry II.*

LEFT: *Castle Acre, in Norfolk, originated as a Norman fortification shortly after the Conquest. The early castle probably included a stone gatehouse, and its defences were greatly improved during the 12th century with the construction of a curtain wall and earthwork ramparts.*

ABOVE: *The stone fortifications at Coity Castle, in South Wales, date from the 12th century and replaced what was probably a timber building on the motte. The rectangular keep and part of the inner curtain wall are the oldest remains. The cylindrical tower was built in the 13th century, and the outer bailey in the 14th century.*

RIGHT: *Situated in a loop of the River Coquet, near the coast of Northumbria, Warkworth Castle has been a defensive site probably since pre-Saxon times. The present castle originated as a motte fortification in the 12th century and was later rebuilt in stone, the outer bailey walls following the lines of the earlier structure.*

Scarborough Castle, in North Yorkshire, is set on an exposed headland overlooking the sea. It became a royal castle in the mid-12th century, after Henry II seized it as part of his policy of centralizing power in the monarchy and suppressing the private ownership of castles. The keep, which was built by Henry II, was originally more than 100 ft (30 m) high.

Tintagel Castle, on the coast of North Cornwall, occupies a spectacular site on a promontory exposed to the full force of the westerly winds. Although there are few remains of the original 12th-century building, enough has survived to show the layout of the castle that Richard, Henry III's younger brother, built in the 13th century.

ABOVE: *Skenfrith Castle – in the Welsh border country near Abergavenny, in Monmouthshire – was built a few years after the Norman Conquest. Except for one tower on the western curtain wall, all the present stone buildings date from 1219–32.*

RIGHT: *William I's military architect, who was also Bishop of Rochester, was responsible for building the first defences of Rochester Castle, on the River Medway in Kent, in about 1090. In 1127, William de Corbeil, Archbishop of Canterbury, built a magnificent stone keep, which was more than 113 ft (34 m) high and whose lower walls were 12 ft (3.5 m) thick at the base.*

LEFT: *Despite its impressive defences and strategic situation on a clifftop above the River Swale, Richmond Castle, in North Yorkshire, was never put to the test of attack. The curtain – which is triangular because of the site's topography – was built in about 1080. The hall predates the keep, which was probably built by Henry II.*

ABOVE: *The keep at Hedingham Castle, near Halstead, Essex, stands in what was once the castle's bailey. Built in about 1140, this severely square keep is in an excellent state of preservation and its four floors show how the interiors of these defensive structures were arranged so as to provide accommodation for the lord and his household.*

ABOVE: *Ludlow Castle, situated above the River Teme, in Shropshire, dates from the late 11th century. Its stone curtain wall contains projecting towers – early examples of the flanking towers that became a standard feature of castle design. These allowed archers to cover the base of a castle wall without using wooden extensions.*

RIGHT: *The castle at Lewes, in East Sussex, stands in a highly strategic location above the valley of the River Ouse. It was begun in about 1069 by one of William I's chief ministers. Unusually, it was built with two mottes, each with a shell keep, and one connecting bailey. While the west motte defended the town, the east motte provided a commanding view of the river.*

ABOVE: *The stone curtain wall of Llanstephan Castle, in Carmarthenshire, can probably be dated to the late 12th century, when the castle came into the possession, through marriage, of William de Camville. A large gatehouse was added in the 13th century, followed by a curtain wall that enclosed the lower bailey.*

LEFT: *The stone castle at Middleham, near Leyburn in North Yorkshire, was built about 500 yds (460 m) from the first motte-and-bailey earthwork and timber structure. The remains of a huge stone keep built in about 1170 still dominate the site, but the town has encroached onto what was the castle's outer bailey.*

RIGHT: *The Welsh prince Llewelyn the Great was probably responsible for constructing the first defences at Castell y Bere near Cadair Idris, in Gwynedd, in the 13th century. The castle is an important example of a Welsh-built fortification. Its location and layout make it a formidable stronghold in the rugged landscape.*

ABOVE: *Although much of Cardiff Castle as it appears today is the result of Victorian reconstruction, the site has a very long history. It was first fortified in the Roman period. The Normans then built a motte-and-bailey castle over the Roman walls in the late 11th century, and added a 12-sided shell keep in the early 12th century.*

RIGHT: *Beeston Castle, in Cheshire, is located on a site with superb natural defences – an outcrop of sandstone that rises some 500 ft (150 m) above the Vale of Chester. Work on building the castle was begun by Ranulf, Earl of Chester, in about 1220, but after his death in 1232, and that of his son in 1237, the castle became the possession of Henry III.*

BELOW: *Defended by a large and imposing gatehouse flanked by two towers, Criccieth Castle, on Tremadog Bay, Gwynedd, was built by Llewelyn the Great. With Castell y Bere (see pages 82–3), it is another example of a native Welsh castle. Llewelyn may have based the design of both these fortresses on other castles in the border region.*

LEFT: *Mitford Castle, in Northumberland, was built in the 12th century in what was then the unsettled Borders country between England and Scotland. It was one of the few motte castles to be established in Northumbria but, in 1215, it was confiscated by King John of England, and in 1217, it was unsuccessfully besieged by Alexander II of Scotland.*

ABOVE: *In medieval times, bishops were powerful lords, as the remains of the castle in Farnham, Surrey, clearly shows. Henry, brother of King Stephen and the Anglo-Norman bishop of Winchester, built the first castle in 1138. Probably destroyed in the 1150s by Henry II, the castle was rebuilt and retained its status as a residence for later bishops until the 1920s.*

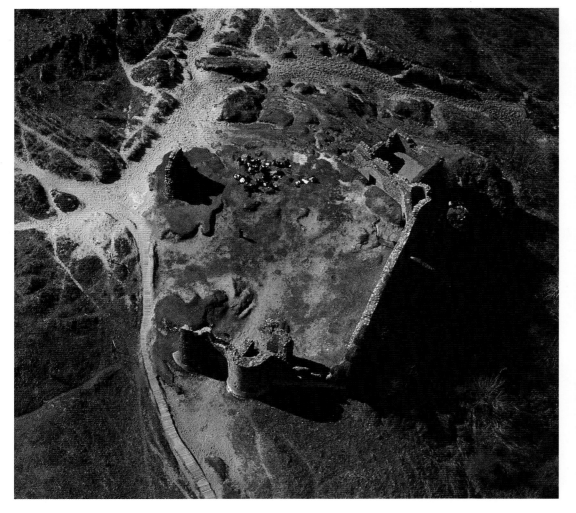

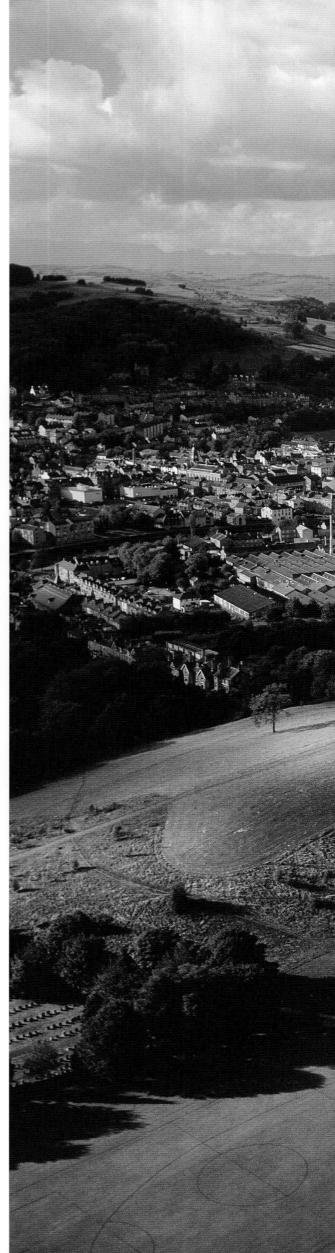

ABOVE: *The final enemy of Pennard Castle, on the beautiful Gower Peninsula in South Wales, proved to be not a human adversary but a natural one, in the form of encroaching sand. The castle was built in the 12th century, first as an earth-and-timber construction and later in stone, but it was abandoned from the 14th century.*

RIGHT: *The sparse remains of Kendal Castle, in Cumbria, bestride a hill that overlooks the town. Consisting essentially of a curtain wall and a square tower, the castle was probably built by Roger Fitz Reinfred in the 12th century, although little about its history is known. In medieval times Cumbria was an unsettled area that was vulnerable to raids from the north.*

LEFT: *Barnard Castle, which overlooks the River Tees, in County Durham, originated as a motte-and-bailey castle in the late 11th century. It stands on land granted to Guy de Baliol and was built most probably by his son, Bernard, one of whose descendants founded Balliol College, Oxford. A sandstone tower was built across the curtain wall in the early 13th century.*

ABOVE: *The remains of Tamworth Castle, in Staffordshire, stand on the edge of the town of Tamworth, itself once a Saxon fortified settlement. The castle dates from the 11th century, when a motte was erected. In the 12th century, a shell keep, which is still in a good state of preservation, was constructed. Later a rectangular tower was built into one side to give defenders an improved field of fire.*

Chepstow Castle, in Monmouthshire, looks down onto the river crossing on the River Wye, close to its estuary. Work on the castle began in the 1060s, as part of the castle-building programme instigated by William I. William FitzOsbern, one of the king's two deputies, constructed the stone keep – still the core of the stronghold.

The ruins of Ogmore Castle are situated southwest of Bridgend, South Wales,
a little way inland from the coast. The castle was strategically sited so as to defend
what was an important river crossing into Wales in the 11th and 12th centuries,
a time when Norman feudal lords were making incursions into the country.

ABOVE: *Carlisle Castle, located above the River Eden, in Cumbria, was a key stronghold close to the northern frontier of Henry II's territory, which stretched south through Britain, across to western France and down to the Pyrenees. Henry retook Carlisle from Malcolm IV of Scotland in 1157. The stone keep dates from about this time.*

RIGHT: *Although much of present-day Bamburgh Castle, in Northumberland, is a 19th-century reconstruction, the landward side demonstrates the medieval principle of a powerful keep – a central stronghold surrounded by defensive walls, with a series of square and cylindrical towers.*

LEFT: *The castle at Helmsley, in North Yorkshire, is surrounded by impressive earthwork fortifications. The banks and ditches follow the line of the stone curtain wall, which dates from about 1200. With two heavily protected gateways, Helmsley was a powerful stronghold.*

ABOVE: *Just above the Channel Tunnel terminal at Folkestone, in Kent, are the remains of an early motte-and-bailey fortification. It is set on aptly named Castle Hill, a spur of the North Downs. Although it is likely that the castle was in existence for only a comparatively brief period after the Norman Conquest, the earthworks are unmistakeably Norman.*

ABOVE: *Berkeley Castle was established at a very early stage after the Norman Conquest, probably by William FitzOsbern, one of William I's generals at the Battle of Hastings. A century later it was in the hands of Robert FitzHarding, to whom Henry II gave permission for its rebuilding in stone, when it became one of the first castles in England to be defended by turreted curtain walls.*

RIGHT: *The aerial view of Norwich Castle shows the impact of the Norman stronghold on the city. Begun almost immediately after the Conquest, the first keep on the huge artificial motte was of timber. In the 12th century, this was replaced by the massive stone keep that can be seen today, and which was restored in the 19th century.*

STRENGTH & SPLENDOUR

*'We have needed 400 masons, ... 2000 less skilled
workmen, 100 carts, 60 wagons and 30 boats bringing
stone and sea coal; 200 quarrymen; 30 smiths; and
carpenters for putting in the joists and floor boards and
other necessary jobs.'*

JAMES OF ST GEORGE, ON THE BUILDING OF BEAUMARIS CASTLE, 13TH CENTURY

When in the 1270s Edward I began his great programme of castle construction on the border between Wales and England, this marked a completely new phase of castle building in Britain. Designed to subdue the rebellious Welsh princes, most of these castles are of concentric design, of immense size and great sophistication, and occupy natural sites – such as coastal or river promontories – that give them formidable strength. By the later Middle Ages, castles were evolving into fortified palaces of considerable splendour. Strength was often sacrificed in favour of greater comfort, such as glazed windows, ornate fireplaces and latrines, which were built into, and therefore weakened, the walls. At the same time, monasteries and bishops' residences, as well as privately owned manor houses were being fortified, the former in response to a wave of anti-clericalism, the latter against the threat of French invasion. In the north of England, where people faced danger of a different kind, pele towers, or fortified houses, were built in their hundreds. In Scotland, where castles had been rare until the 13th century, the nobility built castles to repulse Edward I's advances. Here also castles continued to play a role as military strongholds into the 17th century.

ABOVE: *In 1348 a huge rectangular tower keep was built on the Norman motte at Stafford Castle. Each corner of the keep is defended by an octagonal turret.*

LEFT: *Although it was heavily restored in the 19th century, when many of its apparently medieval defences were constructed, Leeds Castle originates mainly from the late 13th century, when it was rebuilt by Edward I.*

EDWARDIAN SPLENDOUR IN WALES

It was the decision of the great Welsh marcher lords to side with the crown that enabled Lord Edward to win the Battle of Evesham in 1268 and put down the revolt against Henry III led by Simon de Montfort, Earl of Leicester. The crown-marcher alliance also made possible the final conquest of Wales, which began to preoccupy Edward shortly after he became king in 1272. The Welsh were not a formidable fighting power, except as guerrillas.

It was a sign of the times, therefore, that in 1268 Gilbert de Clare, richest of the marchers, began to build an immense new castle at Caerphilly, in southeast Wales. It was also significant that the Welsh made prolonged and desperate attempts to harass the workmen and to take and burn the castle before it was defensible. Nevertheless, by 1277 the castle was finished, and it opened a new epoch in British castle building. The so-called 'Edwardian castles', of which it was the precursor, were based on the combination of three elements: the replacement of the keep by a rectangular or polygonal curtain wall, broken by symmetrically placed towers; an outer curtain wall to provide two linked defensive lines, one inside the other; and the creation of an immensely powerful gatehouse, on the castle's most vulnerable side, in which all the latest defensive technology was installed. All these elements had existed before, but they were first combined in Caerphilly. It is tragic that we possess virtually no documentary evidence (since it was a private castle) about its design and building.

Caerphilly was not only the earliest concentric castle in Britain, it was also remarkable for its size and its water defences. It is easily the biggest castle in Wales, and the terrifically high standards of its

ABOVE: *Bolton Castle, near Leyburn in North Yorkshire, was built by Lord Scrope, Richard II's chancellor, in 1379. It was one of a number of late 14th-century rectangular castles that combined great strength with a high degree of domestic comfort, and included storerooms, cellars, brewhouses and bakehouses.*

RIGHT: *In 1353, William de Greystoke was granted a licence by the king to crenellate the huge pele tower that constituted his stronghold of Greystoke, in Cumbria. Pele towers were defensive buildings capable of withstanding siege in the unsettled border country of northern England. Greystoke was rebuilt in the 19th century.*

masonry and cementation ensure its survival; it is virtually intact, despite slighting under the Commonwealth. Edward I was away on crusade for most of the time Caerphilly was being built; but when he returned in 1274 he undoubtedly visited it and approved of what he saw. In 1276 he decided to treat the indigenous Welsh princes as rebels, and go for an outright conquest, using a series of strategically linked castles of the new type to pacify the territory once and for all.

This inaugurated the biggest programme of castle building in the whole history of the English crown. The programme stretched over more than a quarter of a century, but it was concentrated in three main stages, corresponding with the campaigns of 1277, 1282–3 and 1294–5. There were four groups of castles. The first were the royal border castles of Chester (the king's main sea-and-land base), Shrewsbury, Montgomery and St Briavels, all of which were remodelled and strengthened. Then came three captured native castles – Dolwyddelan, Criccieth and Bere – which were completely rebuilt (other Welsh castles were remodelled). Four new 'lordship' castles – Denbigh, Hawarden, Holt and Chirk – were built; legally they were in private hands, but the building was to a royal design, supervised by the crown and to some extent financed by it. Finally, and most important, there were ten new royal castles: Builth, Aberystwyth, Flint, Rhuddlan, Ruthin, Hope, Conwy, Harlech, Caernarfon and Beaumaris.

Edward was an expert in castle construction, as he was in every aspect of warfare. But of course Edward did not design and build the castles himself. For this he enlisted the services of a man now regarded as one of the greatest architects of the Middle Ages: James of St George, who came from Savoy and who, among other things, had built the castle and town of Yverdon, on Lake Neuchâtel, which strikingly prefigures his later Welsh castles. Edward was impressed by James's work and, when in 1277 he decided to conquer Wales with castles, James was summoned. The ten royal castles built by James vary considerably in design and appearance but they have certain features in common. All had access to the sea or to tidal rivers, to take full advantage of Edward's complete naval supremacy and the economics of water transport; wherever possible, as at Beaumaris, the castles had

(continued on page 108)

ABOVE: *Llawhaden Castle, in Pembrokeshire, is an example of a fortified ecclesiastical palace, built for the powerful bishops of St David's. In the late 13th century, Bishop Thomas Bek rebuilt the old stone castle as a courtyard residence. At the beginning of the 14th century, a large gatehouse with flanking towers was added.*

RIGHT: *Stokesay Castle, in Shropshire, is a late 13th-century fortified manor house – an example of the transition from stronghold to defended country house that occurred in the later Middle Ages. This reflected the desire for a level of domestic convenience and comfort not found in older stone castles, and was also a sign of a more settled countryside.*

CAERPHILLY CASTLE

LOCATION

Caerphilly Castle is located in the centre of Caerphilly, southeast Wales.

HISTORICAL IMPORTANCE

In 1268, Gilbert de Clare, one of the wealthiest of the Welsh marcher lords, began to build an immense new castle at Caerphilly, in southeast Wales. When the castle was finished it heralded a new era in British castle building. It combined three elements – the replacement of the keep by a rectangular or polygonal curtain wall, the addition of an outer curtain wall to provide two linked defensive lines, and the creation of a powerful gatehouse on the castle's most vulnerable side, in which all the latest defensive technology was installed. Not only the earliest concentric castle in Britain, Caerphilly is also remarkable for its size: covering 30 acres (12 ha), it is the largest castle in Wales. After having seen it, Edward I converted the Tower of London into a concentric fortress, then inaugurated the biggest castle-building programme in the history of the English crown, part of his campaign to subdue the indigenous Welsh princes with strategically linked castles of the new type.

NOTABLE FEATURES

The castle stands on an island surrounded by an artificial lake, created by a great screen wall or dam that, heavily defended, controls the input of water from a stream, and also serves as a formidable barbican protecting the approach from the east. An equally large and powerful outwork protects the approach from the west. The castle proper is rectangular, surrounded by two lines of curtain wall, the inner having a tower at each corner and two large gatehouses. The towers project so far from the corners that they command the outside of the walls from end to end. From these, drawbridges lead to the outwork and barbican. The final stronghold is the eastern gatehouse of the inner wall.

docking facilities, or at least a water gate. Secondly, they each embodied new and radical solutions to the problem of defence. At Builth, for instance, the strength of the castle lay in its powerful earthworks, formed by a wet moat and a huge counterscarp bank encircling the whole site. At Flint the design culminated in a great cylindrical keep, built like a French donjon, isolated in one corner of the castle and surrounded by its own moat. Its walls were 23 ft (7 m) thick.

Wherever possible, James adopted the concentric design, which had the inestimable advantage that the defenders on the inner ring could deny access to the outer wall even after it had been breached. But sometimes natural and artificial defences were in conflict. Thus, at Conwy, chosen because it had a sheltered tidal harbour and a huge jutting slab of rock, the natural site for a castle and its attendant town, there was simply no room for James to develop the concentric principle. Indeed, he did not even have room to set up the powerful main gatehouse he normally preferred, and the gateways are simply built into the curtain wall, being defended mainly by the adjoining wall-towers. But this did not mean Conwy was a weak castle. Quite apart from its natural strength, it bristled with traps for aggressors. Access was artfully contrived to be as difficult as possible. On the town side (the weakest), entrance could be made only after climbing a steep stairway, crossing a drawbridge and breaking through three gateways in succession, all in the face of direct fire by walls and towers on every side. The approach from the estuary to the east gate was commanded by a barbican, high above it, and by a tower that stood out in the estuary. The inner gateway of each entrance was defended by a machicolated parapet, stretching across from one flanking tower to the other. All eight towers have beam-holes for wooden hoardings, enabling bowmen to cover every inch of the curtain, and they are linked by a continuous wall walk. Hence this large and powerful castle could be, and was, defended by a comparatively small garrison of 30.

Harlech, perhaps James's favourite castle, was also placed on a superb natural site, for in the 13th century the waters of Cardigan Bay lapped the foot of the immense crag on which the castle rests. Hence there was a harbour built into the crag, so that the castle could be supplied and reinforced by the sea. This was guarded by walls that, as it were, constituted part of the outer bailey extending down the cliff. The approach to the upper fortress from the water gate was a steep path cut into the rock, defended at a point two-thirds up its course by a gate with a ditch and drawbridge, and terminating in a postern gate under the command of the southwest corner tower. The inner bailey is, in effect, a narrow terrace between two walls. On the eastern, or vulnerable, side, facing higher ground, the castle had a very powerful front. There are two drawbridges and two gateways, all under fire not only from the walls and towers in front but from the wall walk of the outer bailey on the right flank. The outer gate was defended by a two-leaved door, and the passage of the gatehouse proper was guarded by a timber bar, three portcullises, two doors and eight machicolations. Hence it was the real stronghold of the castle, and though the wall walk is otherwise continuous, the gatehouse was a self-contained defensive unit which could be held even against a force that had broken into the heart of the castle.

Royal castles, however, might have symbolic as well as military importance. Conwy, for instance, was the nearest equivalent to a North Welsh capital. It was the burial place of Llywelyn the Great, as well as the site of his palace, and it contained a Cistercian monastery that had the status of a nation church, like Westminster Abbey. All were completely demolished and covered by the massive fortification of the new castle and town. Caernarfon was invested with even more symbolism. This was the ancient centre of the kingdom of Gwynedd, the site of Roman, Norman and Welsh castles. Edward's capture of it in 1283 was the culminating point of the war. He determined to build an imperial capital there, as a suitable setting for his royal progresses and as a headquarters for his viceroy, Otto de Grandson.

Hence it is no accident that Caernarfon, though designed and built by James, and in all military essentials following the same pattern as his other big castles, has superficially a very different appearance. The towers are polygonal rather than round, and there is a very striking patterning of the walls with banks of coloured stone. Patterning and polygonal towers occur in conjunction only in the famous Theodosian Walls of Byzantium: it was on this imperial city that the fortress-town of Caernarfon seems to have been modelled. Like Conwy, its site made true concentricity impossible; in fact, it resembles an hour-glass, with a narrow waist and two bulging ends. But it has two splendid gatehouses and nine powerful towers, many with turrets projecting high above the battlements. The Eagle Tower is over 120 ft (36 m) high and has the essentials of a keep, such as a chapel. In fact it once had its own water gate and dock, which meant that it could still be supplied from the sea (which also provided an escape route) even if the rest of the castle fell. Along and inside the walls were two tiers of mural passages pierced with arrow-loops, and on the south side, there were three tiers of fighting platforms. Fully garrisoned, then, the castle had stations for a large number of archers, with tremendous firepower. And the King's Gate, or principal gate-house, though built after James's death, clearly follows his original plan and is the masterpiece of Edwardian military architecture. It was approached by a drawbridge that worked on a pivot between the moat and a pit. The outer passages were protected by four portcullises and two doors, and commanded from above by seven sets of machi-colations. If set on fire, the portcullises could be drenched with water. The entrance passage was under fire from a number of arrow-loops on both sides, and its centre portion was commanded by six doorways, through which heavy missiles could be thrown down. There was also an inner passage, designed to have a portcullis and door at both ends.

Beaumaris, the last of the Edwardian castles, is the tragedy of an unfinished masterpiece. On a flat site with access to the sea, it expressed the idea of concentricity and covering firepower to perfection. Edward must have been delighted with James's design and he pressed the work ahead at a tempo phenomenal even by his

Kenilworth Castle, in Warwickshire, proved the strength of its defences when it was besieged by Henry III in 1266 for six months, capitulating only when the defenders' supplies of food were exhausted. Just over a century later, John of Gaunt converted it into a sumptuous residence with a magnificent great hall, the remains of which survive.

standards. Yet by the winter of 1295–6, the financial pressures were already acute. Work continued spasmodically for many years but in 1343, when the castle was surveyed, it was still unfinished. In its basic structure, Beaumaris is substantially the same today as when work was abandoned early in the 14th century. It has a square inner bailey with walls 15 ft (4.5 m) thick, six towers and two powerful gateways, each with three portcullises and two doors. The outer bailey has twelve towers and two gatehouses, with a dock at the south gateway where the moat meets a 'cut' from the sea. The gap between the inner and the outer curtains is narrow, so that the inner can control the outer; and, in addition, the outer towers are built out of line with the inner ones, thus exposing the flanks of an enemy advancing from the outer to the inner gate. The gatehouses are set opposite to each other, as at Caerphilly; and, as at Harlech, their defences were planned so that they could be held as easily against the inner as the outer bailey. The real stronghold of the castle was the north gatehouse, which could be almost instantly isolated from the curtain wall simply by shifting movable bridges.

Beaumaris was built to palatial standards. It had five suites of noble lodgings. The main hall in the north gatehouse, with its five huge windows (facing inwards of course), must have been a splendid apartment. Naturally the comforts, even luxuries, of these Welsh castles have vanished. But they were once very prominent. Edward campaigned as hard as any medieval monarch, but he liked to surround himself with magnificence and ease, and he took his wife wherever he went.

It is remarkable how much of Edward's work in Wales has survived. He did a tremendous amount of building at Westminster and the Tower of London, but it is concealed by later work. His great religious foundation, Vale Royal in Cheshire, has gone. There is little to show for his titanic efforts in Scotland. But in Wales only his castle at Builth has vanished. Flint, Aberystwyth and Hope are ruins. But Rhuddlan and Harlech are substantially intact, and Conwy, Caernarfon and Beaumaris are complete, so far as the stonework is concerned. They are a testimony to the determination of a great king, and to the skills of a great designer. They also mark the transition from the austere fortresses of the Norman-Angevin age to the castle-palaces of the later Middle Ages.

LEFT: *An early castle at Allington, in Kent, was destroyed in the 1170s by Henry II as punishment for rebelling. The surviving medieval buildings, which include a rectangular curtain wall and a gatehouse, date from the reign of Edward I and were restored in the early 20th century.*

BELOW: *Dunstanburgh, in Northumberland, was one of three powerful castles that, together with Alnwick and Bamburgh, held the key to the northeast of England in the later Middle Ages. Its fortified area – on a strong coastal promontory – covered more than 11 acres (4.5 ha). The castle was modernized by John of Gaunt in 1380–84.*

THE LAST OF THE FEUDAL CASTLES

Like his grandfather, Edward III was a martial man, and a sumptuous, if not extravagant, builder. And like his grandfather, who had James of St George to realize his schemes, Edward III also had his own building impresario, William of Wykham. At Windsor, Edward and Wykham completely transformed the castle, turning it into a splendid fortified palace and installing the latest military technology and domestic amenities.

Edward had decided to enforce his claim to the French crown. In the 1340s and 1350s he was generally successful, but in the late 1360s and 1370s he lost command of the sea, at any rate from time to time, and England's coasts were exposed to attack by the French. England was also growing increasingly nationalistic in the second half of the 14th century, and making the southeast secure was something of a national effort. The walls of coastal towns were strengthened, and a number of wealthy landowners and retired generals in the area received royal licence to fortify their manors or build castles.

One example is Scotney Castle, in Kent, which was fortified as a direct result of the French sackings of Rye and the Isle of Wight in 1377. The ensemble at Scotney as it is seen today contains only a fragment of the 14th-century castle, with a 17th-century house attached. It comprised a formidable defensive area, though on a small scale: the moat was made to circle two islands, where people and cattle could find safety, the eastern one girdled with a curtain and four circular towers, one of which stands to its full height (though minus battlements and with a 17th-century conical roof). There was a similar scheme at Penshurst, though without water. In essence, Penshurst is the finest 14th-century manor house in the country, with an unaltered great hall fit for a king.

Another refortified house was Leeds Castle, in Kent, built at the junction of three roads, and originally with a triple barbican to overlook them. Edward I acquired it in 1272. He remodelled the gatehouse and built a new wall with D-shaped turrets. Leeds is on an island, with elaborate water defences, and it was these that were developed in the late 14th century to meet the French threat. At Cooling, also in Kent, John de Cobham received a licence to fortify his house on the north Kent marshes in 1381 – the French had attempted to sail up the Thames two years before.

In 1386, Sir Edward Dalyngrigge, one of Edward III's generals, was given licence to crenellate his manor house on the Bodiam estate, in Sussex. This is on the Rother, then a navigable river, and thus a possible route of entry for the French. The licence, as usual, provided simply for fortifying an existing house. But Sir Edward found this impracticable. He abandoned his manor, and built an entirely new castle halfway up the hill. Bodiam is one of the best-preserved examples of a late medieval courtyard castle. Sir Edward demanded

Building a castle represented a huge investment in materials, labour and time. The surviving accounts of the construction of Flint Castle, in Flintshire, where building began in 1277 as part of Edward I's programme of defences, reveal that over four months no less than £9 7s 6d was deducted from wages for bad work and absenteeism. The final cost of construction was about £7,000, a huge sum.

comfort and was rich enough to provide it for himself; so the castle had the full range of suites for his family, a chapel, quarters for his men and his servants, and ample facilities of all kinds.

The castle has been criticized on the grounds that the walls are too thin, and not much use against cannon. But in some ways it was an ingenious castle. Rectangular in shape, it had a powerful circular tower at each corner, with a gatehouse in the middle of the north side and square towers in the middle of each of the other sides, the south square tower having a postern. To cross the very wide moat, fed from the Rother, an aggressor had to overcome a barbican and an outwork, both within the moat. The approach was by a timber bridge, at right angles to the gateway and exposed to flank fire from the castle walls. The entrance was from the bank by a drawbridge. To reach the barbican you had to turn right on the outwork and cross a second drawbridge; and from the barbican a third drawbridge led to the main gateway of the castle. Unfortunately, all this elaborate system is gone and the present approach is simply by a straight causeway, probably built in the 16th century. But the castle defences themselves remain: the gateway was defended by machicolations, loopholes, three sets of barriers, one at either end and one in the middle, each consisting of a portcullis and door; the passages of the main gateway (and postern) are vaulted, the bosses of the ribbing having, in many cases, holes 6 in (15 cm) wide, to provide painful surprises for intruders. Given that the cannon of the 1390s were not yet of much use against stonework, this would have been a difficult castle to take in its own age. And Bodiam was only one of a number of late 14th-century rectangular castles, many built by rich veterans, which combined strength with a high level of comfort.

Some of these military adventurers, like Sir Edward Dalyngrigge, were immensely rich. Such men not only built expensive new castles, they also retained large numbers of mercenaries to defend them. It was this practice, which has been termed a bastard kind of feudalism, that was one powerful element in the anarchy that marked England in the middle decades of the 15th century. The old knight-service system had virtually broken down. Neither king nor lords were now followed into battle by men whose relationship to them was based on feudal services deriving from the ownership of land. They hired killers, and then in turn their power and wealth attracted the loyalty and services of neighbours. Of course such a system could only flourish when the central monarchy was weak, and it was precisely in the minority and feeble majority of Henry VI that the country reverted to the baronial gangsterism of Stephen's reign in the 1130s to 1150s. Then the private castles flourished again.

The mercenaries who served these lords were loyal only so long as the pay was forthcoming. This had its effects on castle architecture. Increasingly, the lord's part of the building was isolated from the rest, so that it could be defended against mutinous or treacherous followers. This was true, for instance, of Bodiam, and most of the late 14th-century castles mentioned above; and it was also a common feature of all remodelled castles in the 15th century. Bodiam, too, had a mess hall with kitchen, as well as separate lodgings, for the retainers. Such 'livery and maintenance' lodgings were built by most of the great lords.

ABOVE: *Rhuddlan Castle, in Denbighshire, was one of ten royal castles built by Edward I as part of his campaign to conquer Wales in the late 13th century. James of St George, who came from Savoy, and who is now regarded as one of the greatest architects of the Middle Ages, was chosen by Edward to carry out the huge building programme. He served the king for 30 years, for the payment of three shillings a day.*

LEFT: *Denbigh Castle, in Denbighshire, was another late 13th-century castle and, although it was owned by the Earl of Lincoln, it was built to a royal design. Denbigh had the distinction of having a garderobe, or privy, with a rainwater flushing device. This was something of a luxury in an age when privies were often the only really private places in castles and were therefore recommended as good places to read.*

In some cases the lord felt safer (and could live more grandly) if he built himself a great tower, or donjon, on the French model. At Warwick, for example, two such towers were built, with many tiers of well-lighted rooms, fireplaces, latrines and mural bedrooms. One feature of these towers of 'bastard feudalism' is that they are often made of brick. The finest of them all is at Tattershall, in Lincolnshire. Sometimes, and more in the English tradition, 15th-century brick towers take the form of gatehouses. At Herstmonceux in Sussex, Roger de Fiennes, Cromwell's contemporary and Treasurer of the Household, built himself a large rectangular brick castle (licensed to be crenellated in 1441); this has a moat and high walls, with octagonal towers projecting at the corners and semi-octagonal towers at intervals in the curtain, but the main defences, behind a counter-balance drawbridge, were powerful towers of the gatehouse, equipped for artillery and with a double fighting-platform on top.

Of course these bastard-feudal chieftains were not the only section of society to defend themselves with stone and brick. Society was no more secure in the 14th and 15th centuries than it had been earlier, and in some ways was less so. The later Middle Ages in England were marked by rising anti-clericalism. The Pope was hated because it was thought he sided with the French. Clerical wealth and privilege aroused endless resentment, and many high ecclesiastics were identified with government mismanagement and intolerable taxation. Since they could not be tried in the ordinary courts they were often lynched. So, to defend themselves, bishops and abbots crenellated, turreted and moated their dwellings. Everywhere bishops refortified their own castles, and monasteries that had hitherto been totally undefended built themselves walls. More striking still are the strong, crenellated gatehouses added to the buildings of many English abbeys and priories, which now felt themselves to be objects of possible attack. Hence a great many of the surviving late-medieval gatehouses are monastic. For the most part they were not defensible against an army, but they provided some degree of protection against mobs or gangs of baronial marauders.

It was against such casual enemies that many secular buildings, chiefly manor houses, were fortified or refortified at this time. An outstanding example is Hever Castle, in Kent. Its first licence to crenellate came around 1340, but the moating and main defences seem to have been planned after a further licence was issued in 1384. The three-storey gatehouse is massive, and the building as a whole is well-preserved (and expensively restored by the Astors after 1903). But it could not have withstood cannon fire.

Cannons were coming in, in increasing power and growing numbers. It is a paradox that technology was producing ever-proliferating luxury in castles and, at the same time, ever deadlier means of blowing it all to bits. Carpenters had been the traditional engineers, siege experts and makers of war-machines. But in the 14th century, with the coming of gunpowder, they began to yield place to the smiths, who made weapons of all kinds, although, increasingly, the royal smiths specialized in hand-guns and cannon.

(continued on page 119)

Caerlaverock, in Dumfriesshire, was captured by Edward I in 1300, when it was the newest and most formidable castle in southwestern Scotland. This was a great prize, as Caerlaverock straddled the natural invasion route across the Solway Firth from Cumbria and on into Scotland. Later, the castle changed hands many times between the Scots and the English.

The first cannons were very small, weighing only between 20 and 40 lb (9 and 18 kg). But they quickly grew in size; by the time of Richard II guns of up to 600 lb (270 kg) were being made for use against forts and castles. In England cannons first became of real military importance in the rearmament against the French invasion threat, which led to the castle-building programme described earlier.

By the 15th century, cannons had really begun to win sieges, if not yet battles. But they had by no means yet rendered castles obsolete. Building, maintaining and defending castles had always put a strain on the royal purse. However, a king who, like William I, built a modern castle in every county town and at every important bridge crossing, and had it garrisoned with an adequate force under a loyal captain, was the absolute master. Again, Henry II ensured that all modern castles were either in his own hands, owned by trustworthy friends, or 'watched' by royal strongholds of at least equal power. This system lasted until the reign of Richard II, but broke down increasingly under the Lancastrian kings.

The royal position improved radically under the Yorkists; and it was completely transformed under Henry VII who, by his multiple inheritances, his confiscations and his good housekeeping, acquired for the crown fully a fifth of all the revenues of England – a position that it had not held since the days of the Conqueror. So he and his successors were then able to take full advantage of the political consequences of gunpowder technology. Not only that: they were able to invest in the first post-gunpowder castles, as we shall see. But in the meantime, the castle still lingered on, if not in all England, at least in the north; and it is to the Borders that we now turn.

CASTLES & TOWERS OF THE BORDERS

While England's borders with Wales were the scene of endemic fighting from the time of the Normans onwards, the Scottish border was comparatively quiet until the end of Edward I's reign. This is not to say that castles were rare in the north. On the contrary. In Northumbria there are a great many of all kinds. There, fortified sites date from Roman times; but many continued to be occupied until the 16th century. And, at all periods, houses were being turned into fortified towers, towers into keeps, new castles built and old ones brought up to date. The tendency was to add to the level of forti-fication as the Middle Ages progressed, and the Borders threat grew.

But in Northumberland, the 14th century produced splendid new castles, as well as the refortification of older houses. While, farther south, the concentric castle and its modifications were being developed, up north, they clung to the old-style keep, though they tended increasingly to fashion it into a tower-house. Bigger castles tended to be on ancient, or at least old, sites, where the defences were naturally strong and where wells could be sunk.

On the other hand, we do possess two outstanding and unspoilt examples of great 14th-century northern castles: Dunstanburgh, set on an immensely strong natural promontory of basalt, sticking out into the sea, and Warkworth, which is completely self-contained, and could have been defended for months even if the outer defences of the castle fell.

Of course, we must lament the times, and the misjudgements, that made such structures as Warkworth and Dunstanburgh necessary. Later in this chapter we shall have something to say about the events that led to Edward I's intervention in Scottish affairs, and the consequences for Scotland. Here it is enough to note that the results for the Borders, on both sides, were disastrous for over 300 years.

The consequence of English invasion, and Scots counter-invasion, was the institutionalizing of violence. Raiding, whether for oneself or for the rival crowns, became a profession, almost the only one, as poverty increased and farming for the market became more hazardous. Time made matters worse, not better. Certainly, under the Tudors, English crown policy became systematically ruthless.

Except in periods of total war there was a system of a kind. The entire Borders area was divided into three marches: East, Middle and West. It is significant that wardens of these marches first appeared in the early 14th century, when the whole security position deteriorated. The duties of wardens were similar to those of the sheriffs, but also included national defence, and the administration of the Border Laws, a complex system drawn up by the agreement of both sides, but qualified by many local bylaws. In some ways they were more savage, in others milder, than the common law of either country.

In addition to the raid, which was really a measure of desperation or last resort, there were guard duties of watch and ward, which applied to all hale men. There was a network of beacons and signal stations, controlled from Carlisle on the English side and from Home Castle in Scotland. These were often piles of logs, 700 ft (215 m) up the hillside; or grates suspended from stone lanterns on the roofs of houses and castles. One fire burning meant that raiders were coming; two, coming fast; four, in great strength.

The system depended on the existence of towers or castles every 2 or 3 miles (3 or 5 km). Then a pursuing posse could be collected swiftly. The system radiated from the various big castles. Indeed, castles were essential not merely for defence but to act as prisons. On the Scots side, the strongest prison was the vast and gloomy fortress of Hermitage, a rectangular brown sandstone tower-house that dominated the wildest stretch of the frontier.

But the focus of Border warfare and social life was not so much the big castle as the pele tower, or fortified house, of which there were hundreds. The word 'pele' has caused some confusion. It comes from *pilum*, a stake or palisade, and whether spelt 'pele' or 'peel' it covers a variety of defensive buildings. Originally there were thorn circles, called lodges, for cattle. Then came wooden palisades, with 'bratiches', or timber screens, added. These were slowly replaced by walls of turf and clay, reinforced by timber, with a ditch or 'fill-dyke' around. This whole fortified area was known, from the piles or pales, as a pele.

Then towers of turf and clay, or timber, were built within the stockade – the cattle on the ground floor, people above, in a room reachable only by a ladder. These structures began to be made from stone, a common practice by about 1550. When stone was also used to replace the outer stockade, the area was known as a barmkin, and the tower became the pele.

This type of fortified building already existed in England in the 13th century. But the breakdown of security in the 14th century forced substantial farmers and squires to build many more. An alternative to the stone tower, which was really a miniature keep, were small fortified houses, longer, narrower and lower, and called 'bastels', after the French *bastille*. Such bastels as Akeld, near Wooler, Gatehouse in North Tynedale, and The Hole in Redesdale, have walls about 5 ft (1.5 m) thick, compared with 10 ft (3 m) in many towers. The entrance was by external stone steps, and stock was usually kept in the vaulted basement floor, or pend. South of the border, the typical tower was a solid square mass of local grey stone, 40 by 50 ft (12 by 15 m), and much smaller within. The earlier towers were grander, built of dressed stone, and sometimes six storeys high. But as more and more families found it necessary to build one, they shrank to three storeys or less, and undressed stone was used. There were slits in the walls, or perhaps one window. The essential thing was that the pend should have a stone vaulted ceiling, and thus be fireproof. The next floor was the main one, of hall-dining-room and kitchen, and was reached by a trap door in the vault of the pend, or by a ladder outside. The men slept on this floor, which had a huge fireplace, and a chimney tapering into the roof. The window was shuttered (not glazed), with a window seat or 'shot window'. Above were bedrooms, then a steep-pitched roof, with thatch, or, better, stone slabs. On it was a 'clan bell' or a grid for the alarm beacon. The corners were equipped with stone bartizans, or wooden structures, from which missiles could be dropped or flung. There might be a spiral staircase in the thickness of the wall, arranged as a 'turnpike', clockwise so that the sword arm of the defender, but not of the attacker, would be free – unless he was left-handed. There were often two doors, the outer of oak studded with nails, the inner an iron yett, reinforced by a heavy wood beam that extended several feet into the wall on either side.

Towers and tower-houses are still common on both sides of the border. Even in the 16th century the Border lairds and squires who lived in these little fortresses had a way of life that was medieval in its austerity, though their lands might be extensive. It was rare to have glass in the windows. The walls were plastered and whitewashed and the floors were strewn with moor grass and rushes. Chairs were uncommon and beds were yet to come. Sometimes, in addition to the tower, the owner had a farmhouse for himself, and separate quarters for the servants, using the tower only in times of active raiding or war.

Harlech was one of three castles in North Wales begun between March and June of 1283. By 1286 nearly 1,000 workmen were employed on the site and three years later construction was almost completed. The castle's formidable gatehouse and curtain wall, surrounded by a second wall, is complemented by its defensive location on a promontory some 200 ft (60 m) above sea level.

Generally speaking, from the crushing of the Northern Revolt (1569) onwards, the north of England and the English Borders began slowly to relax their guard. The decisive moment came in 1603, when the two crowns were at last united without bloodshed. To be sure, this brought an outburst of last-minute violence, known as the Ill Week. But James I (James VI of Scotland), though he could not handle the English parliamentary system, was extremely skilful and persistent in putting down baronial brigandage and general lawlessness, and he successfully defused the frontier. He abolished the wardenships and set up a commission, which ordered all strongholds to be demolished.

Farther north still, however, Scotland continued to live in the age of the castle and the tower-house. Long after the Border problem was solved, new and very strong towers were being built by Scottish lairds. For instance, Coxton Tower, near Elgin, set up in 1644, was completely stone-vaulted; except for the door and window-frames it did not contain a scrap of wood and so was completely fireproof. The axes of the vaults were reversed in each room above the other, to spread the stress; and it was complete with a yett, machicolations and gun-loops. It says a good deal for Scottish conditions that in the mid-17th century a man still found it desirable to build a house capable of outfacing anything short of an army; and to Scotland we now turn.

THE SCOTTISH INHERITANCE

What is striking about the historic castles in Scotland is not merely their quantity, but the number that have survived into modern times as well as the high proportion that are still inhabited. To understand the reasons for this we must examine Scottish history.

The eastern coast and lowlands of Scotland were penetrated by the Norman invaders, and their French and Flemish allies, almost as quickly as England itself. And, as in England, they introduced a feudal system based on motte-and-bailey castles. By the 12th century the Scottish ruling class (outside the Highlands and Islands) was almost exclusively recruited from families of Norman, Breton and Flemish origin. The Scottish royal house identified itself completely with the French-speaking nobility and its feudal institutions. The Scottish kings looked to the south and to the southern, foreign ideal. Two of them had English wives, and all had English lands and titles. They created a new monarchy, on Anglo-Norman principles, based on four institutions: the spread of feudalism, the reform of the church on the lines William the Conqueror had followed in England, the plantation of burghs, and the personal royal control of government machinery.

LEFT: *With Skenfrith and Grosmount, White Castle, in Monmouthshire, was one of three Norman castles built to guard routes from England into South Wales. Its name comes from the white render that once covered its walls. It was refortified in the late 13th century, when a gatehouse was built and flanking towers were added to the curtain wall.*

FOLLOWING PAGES: *In 1441, Roger de Fiennes, Treasurer of the Household, built himself a large rectangular brick castle at Herstmonceux, in East Sussex, with a moat and high walls. Octagonal towers were set at the corners of the curtain walls, and semi-octagonal towers placed at intervals in it. The castle's main defences were the powerful gatehouse towers, surmounted by a double fighting-platform.*

Scotland as a whole was divided into 'governed' areas, where writs issued by the king would probably be obeyed, and 'ungoverned' areas, which he claimed in name but could not rule in fact. But the governed areas were being progressively extended. Primitive castles were built as administrative centres, as the Norman and Angevin kings did in Wales and Ireland. At the end of the 13th century, the sheriff was still essentially the head of a military district, enforcing castle-guard, which was the main service due, under feudal rules, from landholders. Royal and baronial burghs were set up as part of this civilizing process, and to provide manpower for the castles attached to each burgh. But until the second half of the 13th century, Scottish kings behaved more or less like the English palatine Earls of Chester. In short, in administrative and institutional terms, Scotland was heading in the same direction as England, although it was a couple of centuries behind.

To some extent there was the same time-lag in military technology. Stone castles were rarities in Scotland until the 13th century. Where wood could not be obtained, turf and clay were used for defensive earthworks and walls. Where stone castles were built, they often occupied ancient natural defences. Such sites, common on both west and east coasts, remind one of Tintagel: that is, a Dark Age defensive position surviving into feudal times almost in defiance of the principles of medieval architecture. Most Scottish castles built before the mid-13th century were simple towers, which were only slowly replaced by sophisticated castles.

Edward I's attempts to assert what he regarded as his undoubted rights in Scotland led to a dramatic epoch of castle building and siege warfare over large areas of Scotland. The gap between Scottish and English military technology narrowed almost to vanishing point, as Edward's repeated invasions familiarized the Scottish nobility with the latest hardware and engineering. At one time all the lowland castles were under Edward I's control, and in 1296 he took many more north of the Forth. That year he stormed and took the town of Berwick, and began to build a new fortress there, laying the first stone with his own hands.

Doubtless Edward's original intention was to repeat the strategy he had used in Wales, and transfix Scotland in a vice of impregnable stone concentric castles, with burghs of English settlers attached. Certainly he tried hard enough, to the limits of his resources. Indeed, the Scots nationalists did not regard castles as neutral instruments of war, which might be held by them just as strongly as by the English invader. On the contrary, they regarded castles as practical symbols of foreign rule, and their usual policy was to slight them. In this their instincts were manifestly sound. Where Edward failed was in the fact that he was too old, and too short of money, to press forward his castle-building policy vigorously enough. Indeed he really lacked the cash to build any new stone castles on the scale of his Welsh masterpieces. He had a French war on his hands too. He was never able to give to Scottish strategy the same undivided attention that he gave to Wales in the 1280s. In Wales he built carefully designed stone castles on strategically selected sites; in Scotland he built mainly in timber on sites others had chosen.

(continued on page 129)

BODIAM CASTLE

LOCATION

Bodiam Castle is located 8 miles (13 km) north of Hastings, East Sussex, off the B2244.

HISTORICAL IMPORTANCE

In 1385 Richard II granted Sir Edward Dalyngrigge a licence to fortify his manor house against sudden raids from France, since at this time the River Rother was navigable as far inland as Bodiam. Instead, Sir Edward decided to build a castle closer to the river, but by the time that it was completed, the English fleet had regained control of the English Channel and the threat had vanished. The castle was never tested against the French, but instead suffered when the interior was plundered and destroyed by Parliamentarian forces during the Civil War. It was only when it was acquired by Lord Curzon in 1917 that its deterioration was halted. The walls were restored, the site was excavated and the surrounding grounds were landscaped, so that Bodiam re-emerged in all its medieval splendour.

NOTABLE FEATURES

The design of Sir Edward's castle was simple. Four curtain walls more than 6 ft (1.8 m) thick and 40 ft (12 m) high enclosed a rectangular courtyard, at each corner of which is a drum tower rising another 20 ft (6 m) above the height of the walls. On the north side is a great gatehouse and on the south a postern tower. The gatehouse consists of two large rectangular towers joined above the entrance way by an arch and overhanging parapet. The latter is pierced with holes through which boiling liquid and missiles could be dropped on to attackers. The development of artillery is reflected in the gun-loops in the walls of the gatehouse. When the castle was built, the ground to the south was marshland extending as far as Rye and the coast. The area of the bank opposite the postern tower may have served as the castle's harbour, as it is broad enough for two vessels to berth.

Piel Castle is located off the coast of Cumbria on an island of the same name, about 3 miles (5 km) southeast of Barrow-in-Furness. The Cistercian monks at the wealthy Abbey of Furness built the castle in the 14th century to protect the deep-water anchorage of Furness against pirates and raiders who sailed from Scotland.

The campaign of 1303–4, Edward's last big military effort and perhaps his most heroic, culminated in the siege of Stirling Castle. Stirling has a strong case to be considered the finest natural fortress in Britain. It is a high, steep rock, with flat country all around, and though it slopes into the town of Stirling – its weakest side – it is otherwise abrupt, the views are magnificent, and its command over the roads and rivers of the area absolute. In his thorough and professional manner Edward concentrated first on getting his besieging army in the right places. For the siege itself the king assembled a collection of mangonels, catapults and other stone-throwing engines unique in British history. There were a dozen large siege engines. The siege began on 22 April 1304 and lasted 12 weeks. Virtually every known method of warfare was employed, including Greek fire and, very likely, gunpowder. For 30 Scots rebels to defy the military might of England for three months seemed to the king intolerable. Moreover, the capture of Stirling served nothing. The new settlement, in turn, was overthrown by Bruce's coronation in 1306 and further rebellion. There followed 100 years of fluctuating warfare, during which the Scots gradually drove the English out of the southern uplands.

Life in the 'governed' parts of Scotland was better and more secure in the 13th century than it was 300 years later. There were many schemes for resettling the ungoverned lands and, during the reign of James VI, plans to build colonizing burghs. But the independence of the Highlands remained more complete than that of Ireland beyond the pale. One chief reason was the incompetence or misfortune of the Scots kings. Many of them came to the throne as infants, nearly always fatal for good government in the Middle Ages. The feudalism that the royal line had promoted collapsed as a vehicle for unity and instead promoted faction. The crown, as in England under Henry VI, was too poor to dominate the military scene. Most of the powerful castles were in private hands. There the nobles entrenched themselves, converting their government offices into hereditary tenures and gradually acquiring inalienable rights of 'regality'.

In these circumstances vigorous and successful families could compete with royalty, and this is reflected in the powerful castles they built from the 14th century onwards. Thus at Tantallon, in East Lothian, the Douglases, Earls of Angus, built one of the greatest of all Scottish medieval castles. It is about 2 miles (3 km) to the east of North Berwick, perched on high cliffs overlooking the sea, a wild and lonely spot. Here, the sea cliffs form natural defences of great power, and the castle's immensely strong gatehouse forms its main building. But in addition the powerful high fighting-platforms on either side of the gateway and the outer bailey with its vast earthworks – which spring vividly to the eye in air photographs – give more than a hint of the grim defensive system of Caerphilly (see pages 102, 106–7). It needs no imagination to see that the family that controlled this castle could hold the road from Berwick to Edinburgh against anything less than a national army.

In the 14th century castles of comparable strength and importance were being built much farther north in Scotland. A case in point is Glamis Castle. Here we have a departure from the concentric-style castle, ultimately of Norman inspiration and commoner in the south, and instead a development towards the huge tower-houses that were Scotland's most characteristic form of military defence. An iron yett still defends the main entrance door at the foot of this stairway, and the heart of the castle remains the great tower, which an independent Scots lord built to mark his growing power in the 14th century.

Cawdor Castle, a new strong tower built in the second half of the 14th century, has essentially the same origins. It is rectangular, on a steep bank overlooking the little Cawdor Burn, which forms the western defence line, with deep dry ditches on the north and east, and the entrance guarded by a drawbridge over the ditch. The original square tower is in the centre, with later ranges of buildings surrounding three small courts. The keep was originally of four storeys, the first and fourth (the two most vulnerable to attack) having stone barrel vaults. Here, then, despite later alterations and additions, is one of the earliest of the big Scottish tower-houses.

Roughly contemporary with Cawdor is Borthwick, in Midlothian, southeast of Edinburgh. In some ways this is the most remarkable castle in Scotland. Begun in 1430, it is a massive two-slab tower, very grim and impressive, overlooking a wild and desolate valley, and protected on three sides by rivers and gorges. It has lost its original curtain walls and flanking towers, but in other respects it is intact. Whoever designed this castle was well in advance of his time; a hundred years later the same principles were still being followed. Despite the simple plan there are an astonishing number of rooms, passages and stairs. It is completely fireproof, all the principal rooms being stone-vaulted, and the topmost vaults are pointed, with a high-pitched stone slab roof laid on top. The stonework throughout is superb, the outer facing being of beautifully squared ashlar. The tower is a good 100 ft (30 m) high, and the walls are up to 14 ft (4 m) thick.

At Neidpath, just outside Peebles and overlooking the Tweed, there is another fine 15th-century tower-house. It has none of the grim beauty and elegance of Borthwick: it is plainly a working castle. Such habitations are not uncommon in the Scottish lowlands and the hills of the south. There is a castle at Threave, on an island on the broad part of the River Dee in Dumfries and Galloway, not far from the town of Castle Douglas. Its builder was Archibald the Grim, one of the Black Douglas Earls of Nithsdale. One can see why he sited it here: its role was both offensive and defensive, since it is on the main invasion route from the south, and was a take-off point for plundering raids into England.

Of course, the Black Douglases were big people; Threave could and doubtless often did accommodate a large raiding party. But every laird, even every bonnet-laird, had his tower, especially in such border areas. Not far from Threave, dominating a little valley south of Castle Douglas, is an excellent example of a minor fortress, Orchardton Tower. It dates from about 1450, and was built for the Laird of Orchardton, John Carnys. Carnys was a man of very modest means and his tower is correspondingly rudimentary. It contains a ground-floor vaulted cellar, a main first-storey room that also served as a chapel, and a two-storey chamber or bedroom. The building served as a watchtower, for the sea could once be seen from its roof.

Carnys's armed followers lived in a range of outbuildings at the foot of the tower, and the whole was enclosed by a defensible wall. At one time virtually every community in this part of the world had such a tower; but over the centuries most have disappeared completely or are reduced to mere heaps of stones.

At the other end of the socio-military scale were the so-called 'imperial clans', like the Campbells, who in the later Middle Ages were encouraged by the monarchy to expand into the ungoverned area. Castle Campbell, their original home, is sited at the junction of two glens in the Ochil Hills, giving it one of the most spectacular situations of any castle in the British Isles. The castle is basically a 15th-century structure, with additions up to the 17th century; and it has a feature not uncommon in Scotland – a late 16th-century loggia in its courtyard, which brings a touch of the Italian Renaissance to this rain-sodden upland setting. Campbell is a formidable fortress, built around a courtyard with the original tower-keep in one corner and outer defences leading down to the glen bottom. The tower itself is particularly strong.

Castle Campbell is a case where increased wealth and grandeur led a rising family to expand its tower-keep into a massive courtyard-castle. This commonly happened to 15th-century towers. In some cases, however, the tower-house did not expand at all, but survived as a residence, more or less unaltered, from the 15th century to this day.

The 16th century was the golden age of Scottish castles, and it is astonishing how many of these were associated with the desperate events revolving around the lives of Mary Queen of Scots and her son James. One of the most famous is Doune Castle. Doune was what might be termed a 'strategic' castle, built on the main road up from

Edinburgh, a staging post to the key western forts at Dunstaffnage and Inverlochy. The castle is a big version of the tower-house type, with a large high-walled courtyard, two great halls and excellent battlements. Mary and James often stayed at Doune. It was garrisoned by the government as recently as 1689, and Prince Charles Edward used it as a military prison during the 1745 rising.

Mary was also at Loch Leven Castle, in Perth and Kinross; indeed, she was imprisoned there. The lake is not enormous – about 9 miles (14 km) in circumference – but it has a certain placid beauty. The castle is on an island close to the shore – not a particularly secure place, since the water is shallow. It is an early 15th-century tower, much added to in the 16th century. Mary was brought here in 1567, after she lost the Battle of Carberry. She signed her abdication here, waited on by the fourth Lord Ruthven, from nearby Huntingtower Castle.

This is a delightful castle, notable for some fine painted timbers, a rare reminder that castles were often a blaze of colour internally. The castle, originally called Ruthven, was the scene of the 'Ruthven Raid' in 1582 when the young James was snatched out of the power of the Duke of Lennox and the Catholic interest. Huntingtower is a good example of the change from the truly medieval castle to the 16th-century tower-house; for its original twin towers, once linked only by a curtain, were roofed over to form one house in early modern times. The 16th century brought greatly increased comforts, even in a late medieval castle like Hailes, another habitual resting place of Queen Mary. The castle is ruinous but the plan makes it clear that comfort was getting the upper hand over security, since there was only one line of defence. All the same the outer walls were 8 ft (2.5 m) thick. This was the pattern: later Scottish tower-houses had very substantial walls, but the actual defences were confined to battlements, bartizans, strong grilles on windows, and gun-loops in the bases of walls.

Scottish lairds not only continued to call their new houses castles, but insisted on making them genuinely defensible until well into the 17th century. For a perfect example of a well-preserved 17th-century tower-house one must go to Amisfield, 5 miles (8 km) from Dumfries. It is tall, narrow, 30 ft (9 m) square and nearly 80 ft (25 m) high, with four main rooms one above the other, the stairs being neatly enclosed in a circular turret. A bigger and more famous example is Craigievar, in Aberdeenshire, an architectural masterpiece in pink harled granite. It can be argued that the tower-house, in its mature 17th-century form, is Scotland's greatest contribution to European architecture, for though its Gallic affiliations are plain enough, the style is unique. At Craigievar, which has over six storeys,

LEFT: The castle on St Michael's Mount, off the coast of Cornwall, is set on a rocky outcrop that rises to 200 ft (60 m) above sea level. Threatened by attack from French pirates, the castle's defences were remodelled in the 15th century, and included several towers and a gun platform.

TOP RIGHT: Haddon Hall, in Derbyshire, is a superb example of a fortified medieval manor house. Restored in the 20th century, its interior, with a Great Hall dating from around 1370, as well as a solar and other family rooms, convey something of the quality of the domestic life that a wealthy household enjoyed at the end of the Middle Ages.

the skill of the designer in crowding such functional convenience and security into a comparatively narrow compass is plain to even the uninstructed. The castle was finished in 1626 by a prosperous laird, William Forbes, known as Willie the Merchant. There is a great deal of fine decorative work inside.

Only in the far north did castles linger on as military instruments. They played a perceptible role in the rising of the Old Pretender in 1715, and if any one action signalled the end of the castle in Britain it came one day in 1719, in the aftermath of the rising, when a Royal Naval ship-of-the-line, HMS *Worcester*, was sent up to Loch Duich, on the northwest coast of the Highlands, to reduce Eilean Donan, the great stronghold of the Macraes. It was defended by a gallant company of Spanish soldiers, but the ship's cannon reduced it to rubble in a matter of hours. And rubble it remained until the 20th century, when a Macrae who had married a maltster heiress spent £1 million on restoring it and making it habitable. Eilean Donan is actually on an island (as its name implies), but it is linked to the land by a stone bridge; and its magnificent setting on the sea loch has made it perhaps Scotland's most photographed castle. But it was the last of the line; the new forts and fortified barracks that the Hanoverian crown built to hold down the Highlands were very different conceptions. And in 1774, when the Scottish author James Boswell and Samuel Johnson, the English man of letters, toured Skye and stayed at Dunvegan Castle, another very ancient fortress, their hostess, Lady Macleod, complained bitterly about its inconveniences and said she longed to live in a more domesticated home. So by then the castle, as a prolongation of a medieval form of building, was effectively extinct even in wildest Scotland.

ABOVE: *For the construction of Aberystwyth Castle, in Ceredigion, in the 1270s, specialist workmen, masons and carpenters were recruited from other parts of the country, including Somerset and Dorset. Problems with the supply of materials and the quality of the work were such that rebuilding was necessary.*

RIGHT: *Old Wardour Castle, southwest of Wilton, in Wiltshire, was built at the end of the 14th century by the 5th Lord Lovel. He created a hexagonal structure arranged around a hexagonal courtyard, at the centre of which was a well. The design was derived from those of castles in Burgundy, although Old Wardour was intended for display rather than defence.*

The earliest surviving stonework of Kidwelly Castle, in Carmarthenshire, dates back to the late 13th century, when a square curtain wall, set with cylindrical towers at each corner, was built. In the 14th century, an outer semi-circular curtain wall, defended by flanking towers and two gatehouses, was added.

Doune Castle, in Perthshire, was built in the 14th century by Robert Stewart, Duke of Albany, to stand guard over the road to the Highlands. Never substantially altered, the castle largely retains its original appearance. It is, in effect, a large-scale version of a tower-house, with a spacious high-walled courtyard and two great halls.

LEFT: *Allotments and back gardens have crept up almost to the walls of Oystermouth Castle, on the Gower Peninsula in South Wales. The castle consisted of an enclosure surrounding a rectangular tower that was built in the late 13th century. Windows were added to the tower in the 14th century, along with a second building. There are also the remains of a gateway.*

ABOVE: *Building at Oxburgh Hall, in Norfolk, began in 1482, as the Wars of the Roses were drawing to an end. Although Oxburgh has some of the features of a castle, including an imposing gatehouse and a moat, it was intended primarily to be a comfortable and elegant residence rather than a fortification.*

In the late 13th century, the defences at Carew Castle, in Pembrokeshire, were completely revamped so as to incorporate the latest ideas in military and domestic architecture. Both the east and west ranges of the castle were redeveloped, the west range receiving an impressive great hall with a huge drum tower at either end. These towers contained private apartments.

Chirk Castle, in Wrexham, North Wales, was built at the end of the 13th century in what was then the unsettled Welsh border country. It was held by Roger Mortimer, who was granted the castle by Edward I. Designed by the royal works department, it was never completed to plan. It closely resembles Beaumaris (see pages 116–17), although it has a single curtain wall.

ABOVE: *Powderham Castle, which overlooks the River Exe, in Devon, was built as a fortified manor house in the 14th century. The medieval building has been absorbed within 18th- and 19th-century extensions, although one of the six original towers has survived.*

RIGHT: *The Neville family, who were responsible for building Raby Castle in County Durham, received a licence to crenellate its defences in 1378. Originating as a rectangular building with a curtain wall and entrance gateway, the castle developed to become a much larger palace-residence surrounded by an outer curtain wall.*

ABOVE: *Eilean Donan Castle, in the Scottish Highlands, is situated on an island at the intersection of three lochs. A fortress was built here in the early 13th century, part of Scotland's defences against Norse raiders. In 1719 the castle was destroyed by bombardment from an English warship. It was rebuilt between 1912 and 1932.*

RIGHT: *Although it has the title of a castle, Weobley, in South Wales, is more accurately defined as a fortified manor house. Construction started in the late 13th century, when a group of buildings were set around a courtyard with a gatehouse. The well-preserved remains of the manor house provide a glimpse into medieval domestic life.*

ABOVE: *Lympne Castle, near Hythe, in Kent, was a residence for the archdeacons of Canterbury, one of whom was Thomas Becket, the prelate, chancellor and, later, archbishop. In the 14th century, a large hall was constructed, and this, together with some early 15th-century additions, form the bulk of the castle's surviving buildings.*

RIGHT: *Caldicot Castle, in Monmouthshire, was built in the 12th and 13th centuries, with a keep on the motte of an earlier fortification, and strong walls with flanking towers. In the early 14th century a large rectangular gatehouse was built. Set lengthwise into the curtain wall, it was flanked by square garderobe turrets.*

LEFT: *The first stone defences at Windsor, in Berkshire, go back at least to the early 12th century. Henry II carried out substantial building work here in the later 12th century and, in the 14th century, Edward III transformed the castle, turning it into a splendid fortified palace with the latest military technology and domestic amenities.*

ABOVE: *Linlithgow, in West Lothian, was rebuilt by Edward I, who fortified the castle on a grand scale in 1301–2, and also turned it into a palace. The work was hastily carried out over a single winter, and to complete it quickly, 100 regular foot soldiers were used as part of the labour force.*

ABOVE: *In the 1370s Sir Thomas Hungerford started building a castle at Fairleigh Hungerford, near Trowbridge, in Wiltshire. The rectangular enclosure that he raised was protected by a stout curtain wall with corner towers and a large gatehouse. The castle was strengthened by his son, who built a new bailey that enclosed the parish church.*

LEFT: *Originating as a motte castle in 1068, Warwick occupies a naturally defended location above the River Avon. In the 14th century, the castle underwent a costly facelift, including the addition of two towers in the curtain wall that contain several tiers of well-lighted rooms for the use of the lord and his household.*

Dating from 1331, the splendid moated palace at Wells, in Somerset, was built in response to the increasing resentment against the Church that marked the later Middle Ages in England. Bishops were often the target of lynch mobs. To protect themselves, they crenellated, turreted and moated their dwellings, as did the Bishop of Wells.

Built by Edward I, Conwy Castle, in North Wales, was a powerful stronghold. It was completed within the short space of five years at a cost of almost £20,000. The castle's walls, defended by eight enormous towers, follow the outline of the rock on which it is sited.

ABOVE: *Compton Wynyates, in Warwickshire, was built in about 1500 as a fortified manor house, with sufficient defences to resist an armed band, but not an army. Its structure probably incorporates part of an earlier building. Designed around a central courtyard, the house had walls 4 ft (1.2 m) thick as well as a moat. It was later extended and embellished.*

LEFT: *Caernarfon Castle, in Gwynedd, was constructed by Edward I in the late 13th century as part of his enormous castle-building programme. The high curtain wall is strung out between 13 multi-angular towers. The castle was part of a larger system of defences that incorporated the town.*

Bardon Tower, northeast of Skipton, in North Yorkshire, is a pele tower built by the
Cliffords of Skipton Castle in the 15th century. Henry, the 10th Lord Clifford, was
a survivor of the Battle of Flodden Field in 1513. He favoured Bardon as a home
where he could pursue his peaceable interests of astrology and astronomy.

*Elton Hall, near Peterborough, in Cambridgeshire, originated as a late medieval
fortified manor house. This structure was subsumed into the residence that was built
here in the 17th century. The building was later extended, although traces of its
medieval origins remain.*

ABOVE: *The surviving stone defences at Laugharne Castle, in Carmarthenshire, mostly date from several construction phases in the 13th century, and include the remains of a curtain wall and two towers. At the end of the 13th century, a gatehouse was added to the entrance of the inner ward, and the gatehouse of the outer ward was rebuilt.*

RIGHT: *In 1296, Edward I granted the Prior of Tynemouth, in the unsettled northern border region near Newcastle upon Tyne, a licence to build fortifications. A curtain wall with flanking towers was built around the priory, and a century later, a large gatehouse with walls 5 ft (1.5 m) thick was added.*

The threat of an invasion from France led the Archbishop of Canterbury to refortify for artillery his old palace of Saltwood, in Kent, in the 1380s. The architect and military engineer Henry Yevele was commissioned to construct a great new gatehouse, with gunslits like inverted keyholes, together with massive water defences.

*The castle of Carreg Cennen, in Carmarthenshire,
was effectively rebuilt after its capture from the Welsh
by Edward I. Situated in a good defensive location,
with cliffs on three sides, the new fortress included
a gatehouse and barbican with a formidable set of
obstacles for potential assailants.*

ABOVE: *Penshurst Place, in Kent, has been described as the finest 14th-century manor house in England. It was built by Sir John de Pulteney, an enormously rich draper who was four times Lord Mayor of London. A licence to crenellate the building was granted in 1341, but although it was later surrounded by a protective wall, it was never a fortress.*

RIGHT: *The threat of casual attack, by mobs or gangs of baronial marauders, was the reason why many manor houses were fortified or refortified in the 14th century. Hever Castle, in Kent, which was granted a licence to crenellate in 1340, is an example of this. Further defences, including moating, were planned after the issue of a second licence in 1384.*

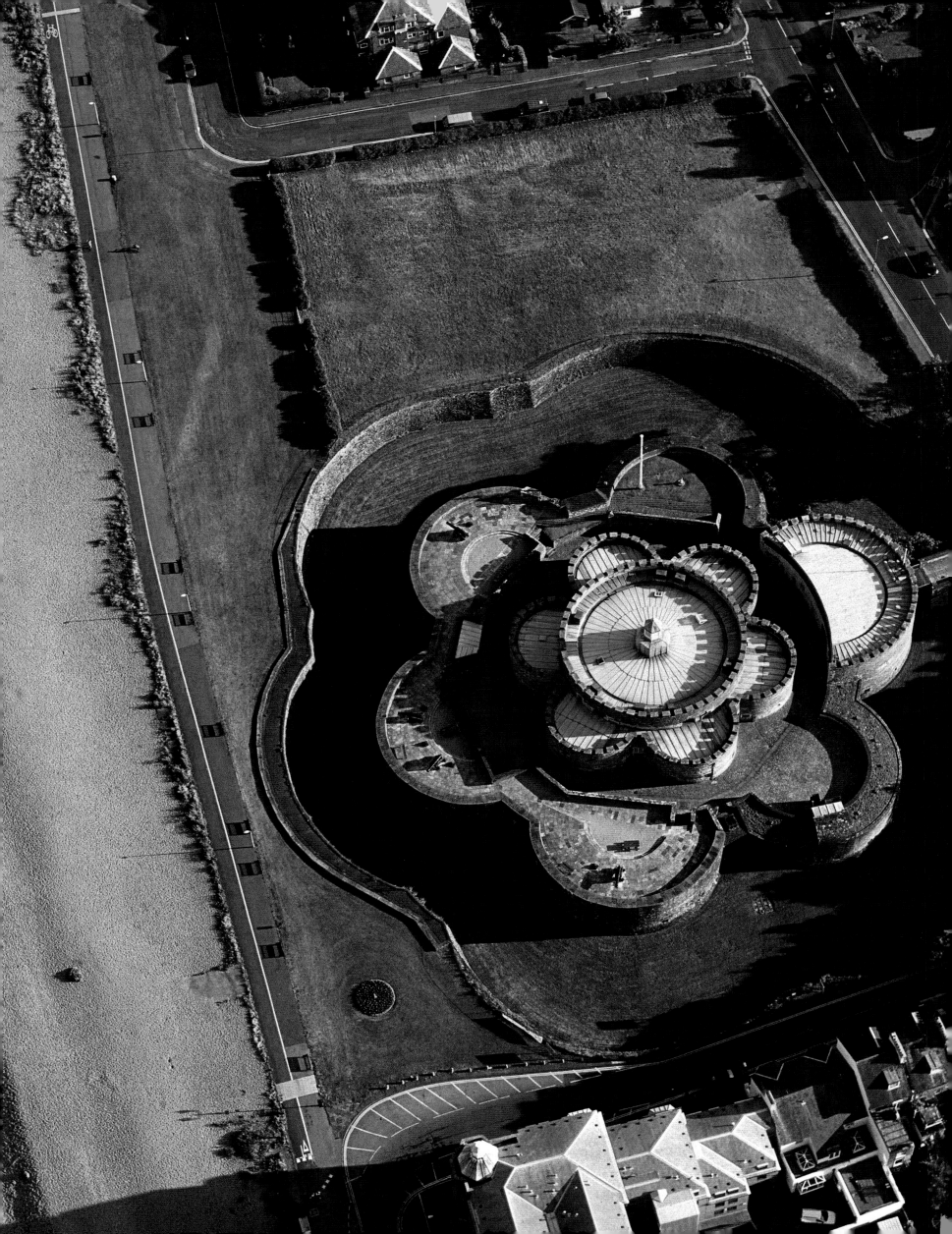

ARTILLERY FORTRESSES

*'The place is ... one of the strongest inland Garrisons of
the Kingdom ... The walls very thick and high, with strong
towers; and very difficult of access, by reason of the depth
and steepness of the graft.'*

OLIVER CROMWELL ON PONTEFRACT CASTLE

The accession of the Tudor monarchy at the end of the Middle Ages brought with it a period of relative peace. Castles lost some of their importance, although they did not become obsolete. They still had a role to play, both as centres of administration and for defence, in the border region with Wales and in the north. But the defence of England's coastline, from Gravesend to Cornwall, was still of paramount importance, in the face of threatened invasion by Spain and France, and for this, castles of a radically new quatrefoil design were built. Exemplified by such masterpieces as Deal Castle and Walmer Castle, these new fortresses were built to resist heavy artillery, and their symmetrical layout is revealed to superb effect in aerial views. The last period of English history in which castles played a central role was the Civil War. In this time of great conflict and upheaval, Royalists and Parliamentarians fought each other from castles and from towns and cities, defended by strong walls. Besieged and relentlessly attacked, many fell, and the victorious Parliamentarians indulged in the practice of slighting, or deliberately destroying, a castle to render it useless. The landscape is dotted with the resulting shells of castles. The aerial photographs of these desolate ruins give a literal overview of a fascinating but tragic period of British history.

ABOVE: *Although she carried out no building programmes on the scale of her father's, Elizabeth I continued to maintain the country's defences. At Upnor Castle, opposite the naval base at Chatham, in Kent, a new bulwark was constructed in 1561–2, thriftily reusing stone from the outer curtain wall of old Rochester Castle.*

LEFT: *Deal Castle, in Kent, one of the artillery fortresses that Henry VIII built in the 1530s, has a distinctive double-clover leaf layout.*

STONE WALLS AND GUNPOWDER

With the advent of the Tudors, the medieval castle made a rapid disappearance from the English architectural scene. In Scotland and in France, the rich and well born continued to call the new houses they built 'castles', but in England in the 16th century, the term was already regarded as archaic.

We find a characteristic 16th-century development (one of many) among the delightful ruins of Moreton Corbet Castle, in Shropshire. Here the ancestral stronghold of the Corbet family, not far from the Welsh border, with a keep built in about 1200, was brought up to date, not in a military sense, but in a strictly domestic one by the addition of a magnificent Elizabethan range. This fascinating essay in the Elizabethan renaissance, dating from 1579, with its five-light windows, Tuscan and Ionic columns, and ornamental metope frieze, is light-years away from the Middle Ages. Indeed, the great new men of the Tudor age – the Wolseys, the Bacons, the Cecils, the Hattons – did not build castles, but instead tremendous houses, like Hampton Court, Burghley, Gorhambury, Theobalds and Holdenby, with only the merest decorative genuflections to the military style.

Yet castles continued to serve a variety of important purposes in the 16th century, and were therefore maintained and even added to in a number of cases. The strength of the Tudor monarchy, and the efficiency of its central administrative machine, made the fortified castle unnecessary and almost obsolete in normal times – inventories of royal castles made at the beginning, and shortly after the end, of Elizabeth's reign tell a tale of neglect, decay and ruin. But the moment the royal succession was in doubt or, still more, actively challenged, castles sprang once again into military life. Thus, in 1553, when Queen Mary's title was impugned by the upstart Duke of Northumberland on behalf of his daughter-in-law, Lady Jane Grey, the queen instantly retired to her great castle at Framlingham, in Suffolk.

Framlingham Castle was, and is, a building of exceptional interest. It was a creation of the Bigods, Earls of Norfolk, although the original 12th-century castle was smashed to bits by Henry II. About 1190–1210, Roger, the second earl, built a revolutionary new castle, with a vast curtain wall laced with 13 strong towers. The new concept, which enabled a large force including cavalry to be kept in the area of maximum defensibility, replaced the type of castle with a dominant keep. It reflected Crusader experience, which itself echoed Byzantine walls and towers, notably at Constantinople: Framlingham was, in a sense, an adumbration of Caernarfon (see pages 108 and 152). The castle passed from the Bigods, through crown possession, to the Mowbrays, Dukes of Norfolk, who made it their chief residence throughout the 15th century, and embellished and enlarged it, transforming the castle and the streets and buildings that surrounded it into a fortified town. In 1476 the castle went through the female line to the first Howard Duke of Norfolk, who was killed at the Battle of Bosworth in 1485. His son, the second duke, pardoned by Henry VII and later the victor at the Battle of Flodden Field, modernized the castle, making copious use of brick. He added the splendid bridge and gatehouse that now form the main entrance, and

he perched on top of the towers a series of magnificent Tudor chimneys, all, save one, purely decorative. Henry VII in his old age imprisoned the third Duke of Norfolk and confiscated Framlingham, and Edward VI gave it to his elder half-sister, Mary. As Mary's chief support came from East Anglia, and as Framlingham's outer bailey encompassed most of the town, thus providing defensible accommodation for an entire army, it was a natural rallying point for her forces. They flocked to join her here, and within a week the measure of her support was so formidable that Northumberland abandoned his venture.

In retiring to Framlingham, Mary doubtless had her own action in mind when she later, during the Wyatt rebellion, accused her half-sister Elizabeth of doing the same thing at her castle of Donnington, near Newbury. In fact Elizabeth was inevitably the cynosure of all Protestant plots under Mary, and in times of trouble it was natural for her servants to put Donnington, the only defensible home she had, in a state of readiness; though Elizabeth, under interrogation, at first denied she even owned the place. Donnington, not yet slighted, was then a formidable place. As queen herself, Elizabeth rarely deigned to lock herself up in a castle even when her life was under threat; during the Armada scare, for instance, she continued to live at her houses near or in London. The only exception was in 1569, when she briefly allowed herself to be persuaded to occupy Windsor (one of her principal homes anyway), which the military experts regarded as the strongest place in the kingdom.

Outside the south and the midlands, and especially in the north and on the Welsh Marches, castles continued to serve important administrative and defensive purposes. The Council of the North, which was a major prerogative system of justice, as well as a military and financial machine, operated from Clifford's Tower, within the vast circumference of York Castle. Ludlow Castle, in Shropshire, was the seat of the Council of the Marches of Wales. It is still one of the biggest and most impressive of British castles. The main gateway leads to an enormous courtyard or outer bailey; in one corner there is a deep dry ditch (from which most of the stone to build the castle was produced), guarding the inner bailey. The inner castle contains the Pendower Tower, where Edward IV's two luckless boys were held before being brought to London; a Norman keep and towers; the magnificent 14th-century state apartments, modernized in Elizabethan times; and, not least, the vast council hall, where the Court of the Marches sat. The castle, on high ground overlooking the left bank of the Teme, was for centuries regarded as the chief key to the Welsh Marches, and has been fairly termed one of the most powerful and complete examples of medieval military architecture in the country. But it is also a complete administrative centre, a sort of miniature Whitehall in the dress of the English renaissance – indeed it was a centre of English culture too.

(continued on page 168)

In 1542 Henry VIII's engineers plundered the stone of Lindisfarne Priory, on Holy Island, off the coast of Northumbria, to construct Lindisfarne Castle, on Beblowe Crag, overlooking the harbour. Lindisfarne Priory had had a long history as an ecclesiastical centre, but the castle was the first defensive structure to be built here.

WALMER CASTLE

LOCATION

Walmer Castle is located south of Walmer, Kent, off the A258.

HISTORICAL IMPORTANCE

The word 'castle' takes on a different meaning with the construction of forts designed especially for the effective deployment of heavy artillery during the Tudor period. In 1538, when the country was threatened by invasion by his two Catholic enemies, Charles V of Spain and Francis I of France, Henry VIII embarked on the most comprehensive defence scheme in Britain since Roman times. In less than two years he had put in place coastal defences running from the Thames to Dorset, to cover as quickly as possible the stretch of coastline where a landing was most likely. Walmer was the southernmost of three forts – the others were Sandown and Deal – built to guard the anchorage known as the Downs. By early 1540 they were in a state of readiness, with wide gunports on the seaward side to enable cannon to be realigned against a moving target. Even though the invasion never materialized, the importance of good coastal defences was recognized and, by the end of the 16th century, there were 10 trained gunners at Sandown, 11 at Walmer and 16 at Deal, supplemented in times of emergency by local men.

NOTABLE FEATURES

From the air, Walmer Castle's elegant symmetry is immediately apparent, its single central tower flanked by four smaller turrets, each with their complements of gunports. Like other coastal forts, Walmer was not built as a long-term residence, but as a base for military operations, and so was not fitted out for comfort: contemporaries complained that the forts 'stank of gunpowder and dogs'. During the 18th and 19th centuries, when it had been converted into a dwelling of considerable splendour, Walmer became the official residence of the Warden of the Cinque Ports.

Until the mid-17th century such governmental castles were operated on the assumption that they might have to withstand a siege; though, as it happened, sieges in 16th-century England and Wales were few and brief. When the Earls of Northumberland and Westmorland rose on behalf of Catholicism and Mary Queen of Scots in 1569, they took Durham Castle without a shot (it was virtually undefended) but failed completely to take Henry II's grim fortress-keep at Newcastle, and their own still-powerful castles were not even defended when the rebellion collapsed in ignominy and cowardice.

Of course, the earls' castles were forfeit; and thereafter the great strongholds on the fringes of the English heartlands, which were still kept up under Elizabeth, served chiefly as prisons, for prisoners of state and recusants. This was the fate, for instance, of Framlingham, of Wisbech in Cambridgeshire and of magnificent Beaumaris. Mary Queen of Scots, during her 19 years as a state guest under house arrest, sampled a number of castles, including several belonging to the ultra-warlike Talbots, Earls of Shrewsbury. Her first proper English residence, in fact, after she was moved from Carlisle Castle, was Bolton, which looks down over Wensleydale, and was built at roughly the same time as Bodiam.

Another of Mary's prisons was the Earl of Shrewsbury's Tutbury, in North Staffordshire, overlooking the River Dove. This huge castle occupied a hill on the extreme verge of Staffordshire and Derbyshire, though by Mary's time it was in bad repair; she said it was 'exposed to all the malice of the heavens'. But in some ways it was a more attractive place than Fotheringham, 20 miles (32 km) southwest of Peterborough, in Northamptonshire. This was originally a motte-and-bailey castle on the River Nene, and later became a prime Yorkist castle after being completely rebuilt under Edward III. Henry VII turned it into a state prison. Catherine of Aragon, in her long rearguard action against her ferocious husband, successfully pleaded not to be sent there; she thought it might be fatal. So Mary must have realized that it was the end of the line for her. The castle had a fine, north-facing gateway, strong keep, a double moat along three sides and the river on the fourth. Mary's trial and execution took place in the Great Chamber.

Elizabeth herself was no castle-fancier. All her life she hated cold houses, and preferred modern homes – with wooden boards, low ceilings and vast fireplaces – to the stone discomforts, however distinguished and romantic, of castles. In her time, of course, much of the architectural idiom of the medieval world, as well as its customs, were being relegated to deliberate antiquarianism, or play-acting. The famous tilts, held on the anniversary of her accession, in the tilt-yard at Whitehall Palace, were elaborately and self-consciously staged by her Master of Ceremonies to conjure up a vanished world of chivalry. Elizabeth was not averse to a castle forming the background to such mumming, provided it contained a modernized suite of apartments for herself. At Kenilworth, Robert Dudley, Earl of Leicester, transformed the castle buildings to suit her taste, and to serve as a staging post on her royal progresses. Dudley was accomplished in all the arts, military as well as civil, and the manner in which he transformed the fortress into a Renaissance palace, without essentially

damaging its martial properties, was a triumph of architectural skills. Kenilworth was a working castle: Dudley kept an artillery train there, as well as powder and a great stock of firearms and armour. But its state rooms and outbuildings could also accommodate the court for lengthy stays. Elizabeth resided there for nearly three weeks in 1575, and was sumptuously entertained, perhaps in a last bid by Dudley to win her hand. The chief feature of the visit was, of course, the water-pageants. But there were also bear-baitings with dogs, fireworks, discharge of cannon, mystery plays and masques.

Nevertheless, stone and brick still had a major part to play in warfare in the 16th century, and castles continued to be built, even under the Tudors, though they were of a radically different sort. As in the 14th and 15th centuries, the motive was coastal defence. But the circular forts set up by the Tudors were built primarily for heavy artillery, and marked an enormous technical leap forward from the crude designs of the mid-15th century. As a matter of fact, the first in the series, Dartmouth Castle in Devon, is pre-Tudor, since it dates from 1481; it was built by the townsmen to head off a French invasion. It consists of two artillery towers, on either side of the haven linked by a heavy chain barrier. These towers had the first proper big-gun ports, 2½ ft (0.75 m) high and 2 ft (0.6 m) wide, giving the gunners a decent field of fire.

Henry VIII took up the new type of fort with his customary enthusiasm. Like Henry IV, he knew how guns were cast, and it is certain that he was personally responsible for the design of at least one of his sea-castles. He built St Catherine's Castle at Fowey, at Bayard's Cove, at Dartmouth, and the Little Dennis Fort, below Pendennis Castle in Falmouth. It is not quite clear whence he derived his ideas. In 520–21 Albrecht Dürer had been called in to advise on the defences of Antwerp, and in 1527, he published in Nuremberg the first known work on the subject of artillery fortifications. This included detailed instructions on how to add artillery bastions to existing walls, and contained plans for an ideal fortress and town. But his gunports were not as advanced as in Henry VIII's later castles. Indeed, in 1532, a Calais document referred to 'splaies' instead of 'lowpes' for big guns, 'which the King's Grace hath devised', and it may be that on this point at least Henry was the real innovator, though in the light of his activity in other spheres it is more likely that he beefed up the ideas of others. Certainly he was keen to employ Continental experts, especially Italians. At the time several Italian cities were rebuilding their defences for artillery; and the Italians were, almost certainly, the first to develop the new science of angled bastioning. But the Scandinavians were also building gun forts in Henry's day.

The big scare came at the end of 1538, when the Pope succeeded in reconciling Henry's two Catholic enemies, Charles V and Francis I; there was then a prospect of a joint Imperial-French invasion, to

(continued on page 172)

Camber Castle, built as a coastal gun battery by Henry VIII in 1539, near Rye in East Sussex, was abandoned just over a century later due to the retreat of the sea, and it now lies about 1 mile (1.5 km) from the coast. Although Charles I ordered the demolition of Camber when it became redundant, the order was never carried out.

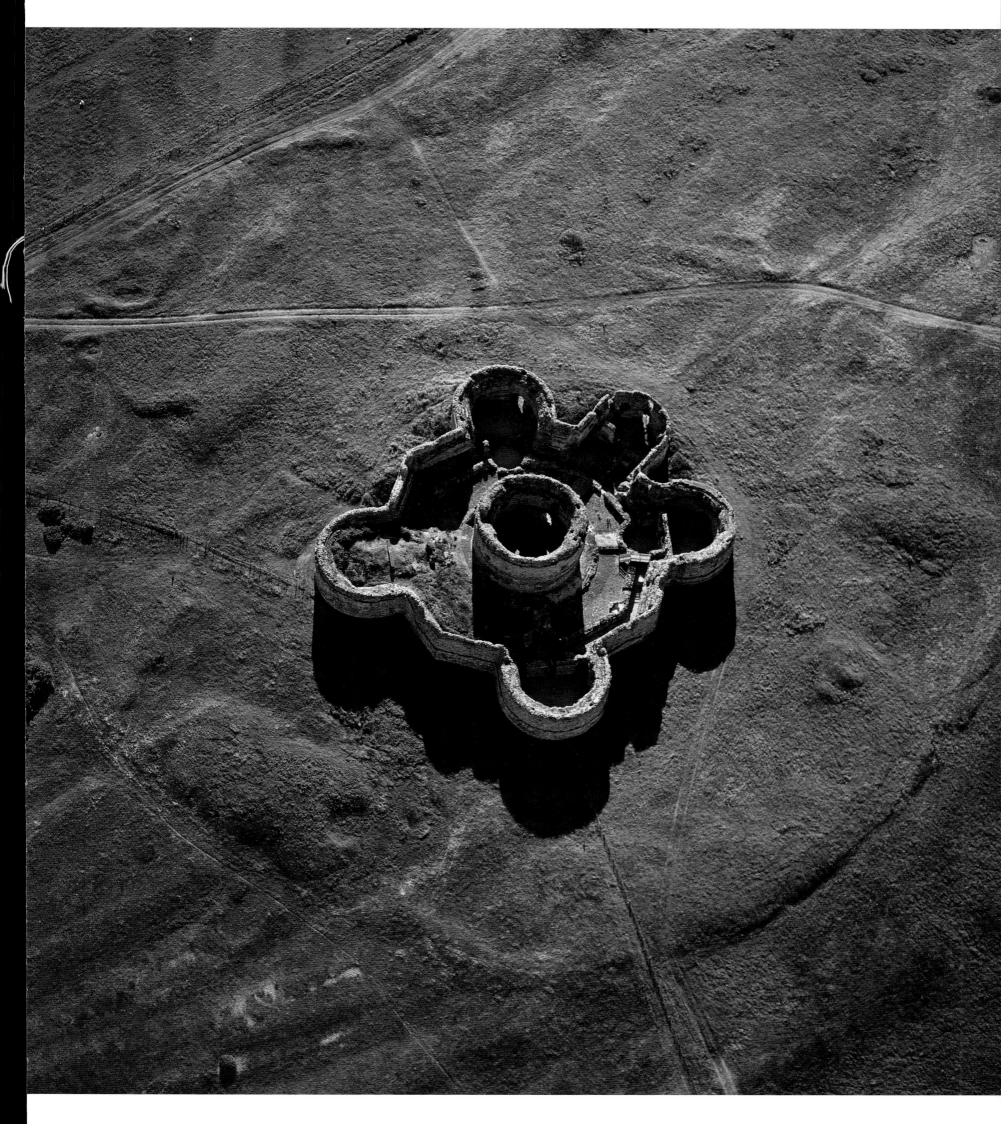

enforce the Pope's excommunication of Henry in December. Whatever his faults Henry was a man of immense vigour and dispatch. In the short space of two years, he carried through the most comprehensive defence scheme in Britain since Roman times.

On the Thames itself he had five forts of bulwarks. Next came the three castles guarding the anchorage in the Downs – Sandown, Deal and Walmer. Next came the 'castle at Floston', otherwise known as Sandgate Castle, near Folkestone. On the other, or western, side of Dungeness was the 'castle at Rye', or Chambre', now known as Camber Castle. Then came the main defences of the Solent, both on the Isle of Wight and on the mainland. These consisted of castles at Calshot and Hurst, in Hampshire, and East and West Cowes on the island. These four forts commanded all the normal approaches to Southampton Water, certainly all those with an easterly wind. But other defences were put up: there was another fort called Sandown (not to be confused with the Kentish castle) and a fort called Worsley's Tower or Carey's Sconce, opposite Hurst Castle, which was modernized at the same time. Of course the largest and strongest fortress on the Isle of Wight was Carisbrooke, with its mighty 14th-century gatehouse.

These forts stretching from the Thames to Dorset were all in working order, if not complete, within 18 months of Henry's setting the programme in hand. Obviously, Henry wanted to cover as quickly as possible the stretch of coastline where a landing was most likely to be made. By the middle of 1540 Charles and Francis had quarrelled again, and the worst pressure was off. But work on the south coast defences continued, at a more leisurely pace, for many decades to come. By 1544, for instance, Southsea Castle, guarding Portsmouth Harbour, was nearly finished; it was 'His Majesty's own device', and is the only castle we can be sure was Henry's own work. At St Mawes an artillery fort was put up to a single clover-leaf plan; but it was sited on the slope of a hill, and so was utterly indefensible from the land side, and in the Civil War, it was taken by Parliamentarians without a shot. By contrast, Pendennis was a formidable piece of work, on a headland, with a flat top and steep sides. It was also provided with a 4 acre (1.6 ha) enclosure or enceinte, straight-sided and with corner bastions; the gunports were arranged to rake all the walls, so making a direct assault with ladders as suicidal as could be. But this belonged to the Elizabethan age, when siege warfare was developing rapidly.

There was nothing quite like these gun forts on the continent of Europe. The biggest and most impressive were the three castles of the

Downs. As a matter of fact their circular shape was not entirely satisfactory. Pointed and angled bastions, giving a complete field of fire to the defenders, were first set up in the Portsmouth area, and 'eared' bastions of the true Italian form appeared at Yarmouth Castle, in the Isle of Wight, around 1547, right at the end of Henry's reign.

Deal is the most impressive of the forts and by far the best preserved in its original shape, though the present battlements date from 1732. It had a clover-leaf design, like St Mawes, only doubled. The linked defence system of the castles allowed them to reinforce and reprovision each other, and thus saved manpower and money; and, in addition, they were brilliantly designed to emphasize mobility within each unit, for reinforcing and re-ammunitioning the defences on each sector. Thus at Deal great ingenuity went into the construction of a central tower, or hollow pillar, with a water-well below, and a double set of staircases above. The garrison was a mere captain and 24 other ranks; but the firepower the castle could provide was formidable. The main armament was mounted on the outer ring, but guns were also fired from the top of the keep, and the inner bastions or lunettes attached to it. Altogether, there were five tiers of gunports or embrasures, and there can have been few more strongly defended citadels in any period.

Walmer was similar in plan to Deal, but smaller; and Sandown, which has now almost totally disintegrated into the sea, had a Walmer-type plan. We do not know what guns they had in Henry's day; but in 1597, at Walmer, there were one cannon, one culverin, five demi-culverins, a saker, a minion and a falcon. Since we know from contemporary evidence that the saker had a range of 1 mile (1.5 km), and a cannon 1½ miles (2.5 km), the guns effectively covered the Downs anchorage. Deal is preserved almost as Henry built it and the sheer beauty of its functionalism makes it one of the most fascinating castles in Europe.

The Tudors were also active farther north in England, for fear of the Scots was acute until the 1580s, and there was always a chance of their descending on Carlisle, or on the northeast coast in conjunction with the French (and later the Spanish). Henry VIII was at Hull in October 1540, inspected the defences, and ordered a castle and two blockhouses to be erected at once. These were of a new, Italian design with curtain projections that were neither circular nor curved towers, but solid, angular structures of earth revetted with stone – and they can thus be considered the first modern forts in England. The king also built forts at Langer Point (now Landguard fort), opposite Harwich, and in 1542 on Beblowe Crag, on Lindisfarne (or Holy Island), in Northumbria.

Although Tudor defensive operations were dominated by the prodigious activities of Henry VIII, they should be seen as a whole, since separate monarchs tended to carry through programmes initiated by their predecessors. Elizabeth's greatest military work, however, was the refortification of Berwick. This was the first English town to be equipped with the new bastions built according to Italian principles. The Elizabethan defences are still in a remarkable state of preservation. By the standards of the day they were very formidable. They have a very thick curtain and huge angular bastions, spaced at

PREVIOUS PAGES: St Mawes Castle, a 16th-century artillery fort on the south coast of Cornwall, sits snugly within its bastions. Although its single quatrefoil design gave it significant firepower, its location on the slope of a hill made it indefensible on the landward side. During the Civil War it was taken by Parliamentarian troops without a shot being fired.

RIGHT: While Henry VIII was building sophisticated forts to match improvements in artillery in the mid-16th century, manor houses in the style of old-fashioned medieval castles were still being constructed elsewhere in the country. Oxwich Castle, on the Gower Peninsula in South Wales, is one such example. It was built by Sir Rice Mansel and his son.

Seen from the air, the alterations made to Carisbrooke Castle, on the Isle of Wight, in the 1590s are clearly discernible. Elizabeth I's favourite military architect, the Italian engineer Federigo Gianibelli, was responsible for the angular bastions and ramparts designed to update Carisbrooke's defences against possible invasion.

intervals; all the bastions have flankers, that is, two-storey chambers in the flank, in which guns were mounted to rake the ditch. Guns were also, of course, mounted on the tops of the bastions.

The fort most closely associated with Elizabeth herself is at Tilbury. Here Henry VIII had built a D-shaped blockhouse at the crucial point where the Thames narrows to a mere 800 yards. Hastily reconstructed and enlarged in 1588, it became the focus of the great armed camp that the Earl of Leicester, appointed head of the army, assembled in the summer, and which Elizabeth addressed in her most famous speech. But it should be noted that the fortifications at Tilbury, which still exist, are more modern works built in 1670, after the naval defences of London were exposed as inadequate in the Dutch wars. Other Elizabethan forts fared better in the 17th century. Pendennis, in fact, proved virtually impregnable during the Civil War, with only literal starvation compelling surrender.

The crown continued to build fortifications of a sort to defend Britain's sea coasts until World War II. But they gradually ceased to be classifiable, even under the loosest definition, as castles. Perhaps the last great working castle to be built was Fort George (about 1770), guarding the approach to the Murray Firth, in Highland. Not only a full-scale barracks, Fort George was also a huge and up-to-date artillery fortress. The motive behind its construction was yet another French invasion scare, that of 1759. In the event, the last period in which British castles and fortresses were to see action on a considerable scale was the Civil War.

CASTLES & SIEGES OF THE CIVIL WAR

The great English Civil War of the 1640s was the last age of the military castle in Britain. Medieval castles, ancient town walls and even strongly built mansions proved surprisingly defensible. What was new were the complicated 'lines of circumvallation' and earthwork bulwarks and bastions that were more or less scientifically thrown up around these strongpoints. If the 16th century had been the age of the Italian military engineers, during the 17h century it was the Dutch (and later the French) who took the lead. From their experiences during the long war of sieges against the Spanish army in the Netherlands, Dutch experts had effectively tilted the balance in favour of the defender, and during the Civil War they were in considerable demand on both sides.

In some ways siege techniques had not changed all that substantially since the Middle Ages. The big works created by the besiegers were, in purpose and design, not unlike the malvoisins of Philip Augustus and Richard Coeur de Lion; and medieval-style siege towers, known as sows, were actually used on several occasions. Guns were less effective than was generally expected. They failed to dominate field actions because of their slow rate of fire and poor traction. In sieges, of course, they could be deadly in the hands of a real expert. They could make a breach even in very stout defences.

Guns, however, were not much use against fixed defences at extreme range. Mortars, which fired crude shells or grenades, were on the whole more feared by defenders than cannon; they caused more casualties. But guns of any size were not common. Ammunition too was less of a problem. In August 1641 parliament had abolished the royal monopoly in the manufacture of gunpowder. When the war began powder mills were set up wherever necessary. All that was needed was to extract and refine the saltpetre from 'earth' found in decomposing organic matter, in cattle sheds, sheep pens, dovecotes and so forth, blending it with charcoal and brimstone, and milling the mixture finely. The process was dangerous but not exactly difficult.

Earlier in the war, the Royalists had a distinct advantage in siege work, both offensive and defensive, for they had many more English and foreign veterans and, in particular, hired the services of the Dutchman Bernard de Gomme, the greatest military engineer of the age, who built many of their greatest systems. Ideally, according to the best Dutch thinking, a defended town or castle ought to have a complete circumvallation, with bastions at regular intervals, plus detached works, or satellite forts, in advance of the main line. Towns with continuous bastion systems included the naval bases of Portsmouth and Hull. Gomme set up a new, and very strong, Dutch system at Oxford; parliamentary leaders thought it the strongest fortified town in the kingdom, though there are virtually no traces of it today. Gomme planned a similar system at Liverpool, but shortage of cash prevented it from being completed. Reading had a continuous enceinte (punctuated by the river), though with only a few bastions. But it had a fine advance fort. Probably the best 'detached work' was the Queen's Sconce at Newark, with its elaborate bastions, a castle in itself. Other towns with continuous enceintes were Carmarthen and Bridgwater. There was another at Bristol, built by Parliamentarians, with artillery bastions.

There were alternatives to the complete enceinte on 'scientific' lines. Bastions could simply be added to medieval walls, and forts were made out of medieval portions of a city's defences, linked with a bank and ditch, or bastions and ravelins added. There were also a number of forts or castles built at isolated strategic points, to guard road junctions, river crossings and so on. Much cogitation and argument went into the best types of defence. One point of contention was the relative merit of wet and dry moats.

Generally speaking the Royalists had the best of it, at any rate for the first two years of the Civil War. There is little doubt that the best-defended city in the whole theatre of war was Oxford, for much of the time Charles's headquarters. Of course Oxford had had a strong castle since early Norman times. When the king decided to circumvallate Oxford, the Royalist experts, led by Gomme, virtually ignored the old walls, except as inner defences, and pushed out the lines to keep cannon shot as far from the town centre as possible. The Oxford defences may be said to have served their purpose completely, in that they successfully deterred a mass attack; the city remained inviolate until the king's cause was lost.

It was at Newark, the strongest royal city after Oxford, that the defences were really tested. This city, on the River Trent, had been regarded as a strategic one since very early times; it marked the point where two great prehistoric routes intersected a river crossing. There were Roman defence works at two places, later superseded

(continued on page 179)

CORFE CASTLE

LOCATION

Corfe Castle is located 6 miles (10 km) southwest of Wareham, Dorset, on the A351.

HISTORICAL IMPORTANCE

Perched on a precipitous hilltop, the broken-backed silhouette of Corfe Castle is a grim reminder of the cruel vengeance exacted by Oliver Cromwell on his enemies' castles during the Civil War (1642–8). Founded in the late 11th century and greatly enlarged in the 13th, Corfe Castle was one of the most secure strongholds in the kingdom, and it was used as a royal residence as well as an arsenal. In the 1630s, the castle was bought by Sir John Bankes, a supporter of the Royalist cause, and inhabited by his wife. Corfe Castle, luxuriously furnished, but with inadequate defences, was besieged by Parliamentarian forces in 1643, and again in 1645, after Bankes's death. On both occasions Lady Bankes refused to surrender and held out despite the attackers' superior military strength. On one occasion during the first siege, Lady Bankes, her daughters, serving women and a handful of soliders managed to beat off an attack by dropping stones and hot embers over the walls. The castle finally fell due to betrayal, when one of the officers of the garrison deserted the Royalist cause. The possessions of Lady Bankes and her family were plundered, although she and her children were permitted to leave the castle unharmed. The castle's fate was sealed when the House of Commons voted to 'slight' Corfe Castle, and the great stronghold was effectively demolished.

NOTABLE FEATURES

The earliest structures at Corfe Castle are near the top of the hill. A large rectangular tower was constructed here in the early 1100s. Later, King John, whose favourite castle it was, built an undefended house – the gloriette – in the inner bailey.

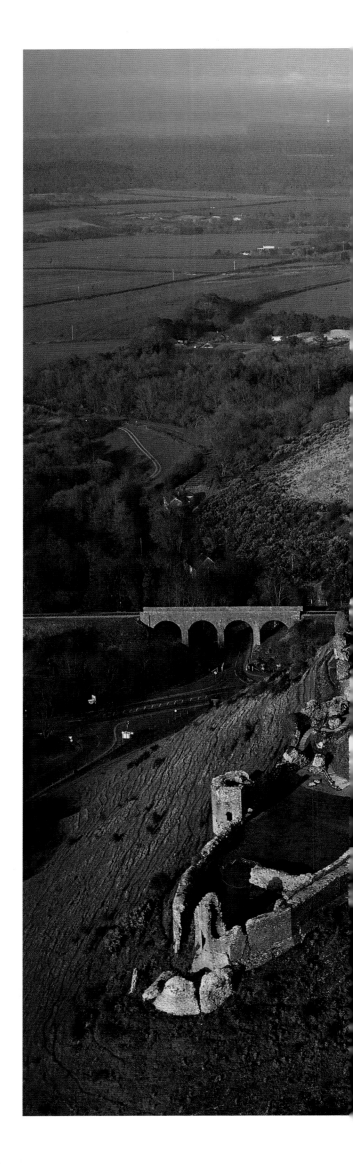

around 900 by the 'New Work', from which the town got its name, set up against the Danes. Early in the 12th century, the town and manor went to the Bishops of Lincoln, who built a fine stone castle, described by Henry of Huntingdon in 1138 as magnificent and of very ornate construction. Occupying a commanding position overlooking the river, bridge and road, it was added to and strengthened throughout the Middle Ages and beyond, and in the 17th century, it was still one of the largest and most powerful river-castles in the kingdom. At the end of 1642 the king's generals decided to garrison and fortify Newark to the greatest possible strength, to make it, in fact, the centre of a large fortified area, used as a rallying point for armies and as a supply centre. Newark Castle, and its defensive system, was linked to other Royalist castles in the area, such as Belvoir, all of them garrisoned. The defensive zone was used to milk a huge area of supplies and manpower, and to mount cavalry raids into neighbouring Parliamentary territory. Parliamentarians made three major attempts to take the city, which finally fell to them in 1666.

One other respect in which the Royalists, initially at least, enjoyed a huge advantage over their opponents was in their possession of a large number of fortified dwellings and castles. Properly garrisoned and provisioned, they could cause a surprising amount of trouble, especially if they were provided with even quite primitive earthworks, to keep the besiegers' cannon from firing point-blank at the walls and towers.

Two castles that gave Parliamentarians enormous trouble were Donnington, Elizabeth's old 14th-century stronghold, and Basing House, near Basingstoke, the ancestral home of the Marquess of Winchester. Both survived for most of the war on the borders of an area otherwise dominated by Parliamentarians, and impeded the advance and communications of their armies. As it commanded the Bath–London road, Charles decided to fortify Donnington in September 1643, with a complete set of 'star' earthworks round it. After several failed attempts, in which hundred of lives were lost and quantities of ammunition expended, Donnington fell to the Parliamentarians in 1646, when a giant mortar blew a hole in the staircase tower of the gatehouse.

The end of Basing House was less satisfactory. This enormous place, reckoned in Tudor times to be the largest private house in England, was originally a motte and bailey built in the 11th century. During the Civil War, Basing was fortified with a complete set of earthworks, some traces of which remain, outside and to the south of the ditches surrounding the medieval curtain. It was owned by John Paulet, the fifth Marquess of Winchester, who was a very pious Roman Catholic and a fanatical supporter of Charles I. He was said to have scratched *Aimez loyauté* ('Stay loyal') on every window in the house with a diamond. He made Basing, on the main West Road, 'the onlie rendezvous for the Cavaliers and Papists thereabouts'. Paulet

Bolsover Castle, in Derbyshire, was built in the 17th century, replacing a medieval fortress that had stood on the site since the 12th century. The creation of two generations of the ambitious Cavendish family, this new mansion included a riding school, a range of state rooms and a gallery 220 ft (67 m) long.

refashioned the defences, building a complete set of earthworks, some traces of which remain, outside and to the south of the ditches surrounding the medieval curtain.

Basing was an object of peculiar detestation to the Puritans. It was also said to be stuffed with treasure and Papist priests. Cromwell finally determined to put an end to the nuisance in October 1645. He had five 'great guns', two of these demi-cannons, one a whole cannon, and two culverins; these guns could breach holes in any building. (At Sherborne a similar siege train under Fairfax had breached the castle in two days; at Winchester, they had made, in a single day, a breach in the wall wide enough for 30 men to enter.) He attacked from both sides and carried the castle at the point of the sword. In such circumstances quarter was rarely given. One of his officers killed a Royalist major in cold blood, saying: 'Cursed be he that doeth the Lord's work negligently.' A quarter of the garrison, including six priests and a woman, were slaughtered. Cromwell's chaplain called the interior 'fit to make an emperor's court'. The cellars were broached, and drunken soldiers accidentally set fire to the house. Coldly, Cromwell had the magnificent structure 'knocked down and utterly slighted'.

There was a somewhat similar tale, though happily no indiscriminate slaughter, at Raglan Castle, in Monmouthshire, the last of the great aristocratic homes to fall. This castle-palace of the Somersets, Earls of Worcester (and later Dukes of Beaufort) was the centre of a vast estate. The earl, a fanatical Royalist, took a number of precautions before the castle was invested. He had the trees in the home park cut down. He burnt down cottages in the line of fire. The fireplace and panelling in the best oak parlour were taken down and sent to one of his lesser houses. Unfortunately he did not remove the library. As to siege-works, he built a battery 500 yds (455 m) northeast of the castle gatehouse, in the style recommended in official artillery handbooks; and he created an entirely new bastioned enceinte, covering the south, east and north sides of the castle, where attack was most expected. By 1646, it was clear that the king's cause was lost, and other garrisons were freely submitting. A siege was, in fact, unnecessary, but Worcester refused to yield. The daily bombardment that the castle then received made little impression on the Great Tower, beyond destroying its battlements, but they did immense damage to other parts, and mortars killed and wounded many before Worcester finally surrendered.

Raglan Castle was 'the first fortified and the last rendered', for Pendennis Castle, in Falmouth, had fallen two days before. The garrison were treated with great leniency, considering the 11-week siege. But Worcester himself was detained in Parliamentary custody, and died a few months later. The castle was slighted, although the Great Tower caused some trouble to the slighters: 'The Great Tower, after tedious battering the top thereof with pickaxes, was undermined, the weight of it propped with the timber, whilst the two sides of the six were cut through: the timber being burned it fell down in a lump, and so still firmly remains to this day.' It is interesting that the Parliamentarians, in dealing with a superb piece of masonry like this tower, could think of nothing better than the old mining technique that had been used by medieval siege-engineers – and fortunate, too, for enough was left, and still remains, to give the visitor a strong idea of its former strength and magnificence.

The victorious Parliamentarian armies slighted the castles that they stormed or that surrendered to them partly because the very existence of such strong points on balance favoured the royal interest; but partly also because the general public mood was hostile to castles, symbols of 'the Norman yoke' and of feudal services – now at last abolished in law by the Long Parliament – and of the expensive and cruel habits of an over-privileged aristocracy. Hence castles were demolished or rendered uninhabitable or indefensible even when there was no warrant from military necessity. Monmouth, the superb marcher castle in whose Great Tower Harry of Monmouth, the future Henry V, had been born, was another property of the Somersets. It surrendered peacefully to Morgan in 1646, but was nevertheless largely destroyed the following year, the townspeople joining enthusiastically in putting down the Great Tower and other strongpoints. At Montgomery, once the key to the central sector of the Welsh Marches, there seems to have been no fighting. Indeed, its owner, Lord Herbert of Cherbury, had built a new house within the walls of the old castle, already crumbling, in what had been the middle ward. The castle was neither defensible nor garrisoned. Nevertheless, in 1649 Parliamentarian commissioners ordered its destruction.

Most people were glad to see the castles go. Even in 1660, when the whole ghastly business of the Civil War and its aftermath was over, opinion was still in favour of pulling down castles. At Caernarfon a demolition order was made, the local authorities agreeing, 'conceiving it to be for the great advantage of ourselves and posterity to have the Castle of Caernarvon and the strengths thereof demolished'. A hundred years later, when the first 'romantic' tourists began to arrive, the city fathers were mighty glad that, for some reason, the order was never carried out!

Where the Parliamentarian generals were undoubtedly justified in tearing down walls and towers was during what Cromwell called the wholly 'mischievous' and unnecessary Second Civil War. For in these cases the castles that defied parliament were commanded by officers who had broken their oaths, and turned their coats in order to put up a futile fight for royalty. Cromwell, who was heavily involved in this business, was particularly angry that men who had taken parliament's shilling should now provoke the terrible hardship and bloodshed involved in storming heavily defended fortresses.

At Pembroke, with its gigantic round keep, one of the strongest castles in the Commonwealth, Cromwell had a great deal of trouble during a siege that lasted seven weeks. Pembroke was not battered into surrender. It gave in because the food was down to 'a little bisquit' and because, by means of treachery within the garrison, Cromwell was able to block the route to the castle's water supply.

In 1592, Sir Walter Raleigh, who at the time was briefly in favour with Elizabeth I, was granted the title of Sherborne Castle, in Dorset. After an attempt to modernize the 12th-century castle, he built a solid new residence nearby on the site of a hunting lodge. Later accused of treason, Raleigh was executed in 1618.

At Pembroke Castle, Cromwell did not trouble himself with trying to knock down the Great Tower, which might well have proved an even tougher nut than Raglan; but he brought down the outer walls and towers. Chepstow Castle was made over to him by Parliament, so he left it intact and garrisoned it. The castle was finally dismantled as a military base in 1690.

Cromwell was even more enraged by the stout resistance put up by Pontefract, the great 13th-century Yorkshire stronghold, with its quatrefoil keep. He wrote to the Speaker: 'The place is very well known to be one of the strongest inland Garrisons of the Kingdom. Well watered; situated upon a rock in every part of it, and therefore difficult to mine. The walls very thick and high, with strong towers; and, if battered, very difficult of access, by reason of the depth and steepness of the graft.' Cannon proved useless; so did proffered bribes; and after a continuous siege of 12 months the castle surrendered only because its supplies were gone and the execution of the king had made resistance pointless. In this case the slighting was carried out regardless of cost and with a thoroughness that left only a chunk of walling at the base of the tower, and fragments of the curtain.

The most important siege of the Second Civil War, and the only one comparable in scale to Newark, was at Colchester. There, over ten weeks, a major battle raged, for the Royalist commanders had managed to concentrate in the town a force of 4,000 men, of whom 2,500 were well armed, and 600 were cavalry. Colchester, of course, was the oldest defended town in Britain, and it was perhaps appropriate that it should be the scene of the last great British siege. Ditches were dug, defending forts built, and the Balkerne Gate, originally a Roman triumphal arch, later a Roman defended gatepost, was turned into an artillery bastion. The Parliamentarians brought a siege train of 40 guns from London. There were several desperate sorties, and much slaughter. Some 186 houses were destroyed and hundreds more damaged by the artillery bombardment. The Colchester people were anti-Royalists, but helpless before such a large garrison. By mid-August 1648, food had run out, and the townsfolk begged the Royalist commanders to surrender.

How many castles in all were slighted by the Parliamentarian forces is hard now to discover exactly: it was probably about 50 or 60. Few complained. When the monarchy was restored, it proved scarcely less ruthless. Many other royal castles simply went out of service and were allowed to decay. And, everywhere, the stone and lead thieves moved over the ruins, an antlike army, working away industriously for decades, to remove the traces of the Middle Ages. But, such being the perversities and contradictions of human nature, while this work of erosion was still proceeding, a few men of means were beginning a movement to reinvigorate the medieval castle in a new, and less objectionable, form.

With its eight projecting bastions, the artillery fortress of Star Castle, on St Mary's, in the Isles of Scilly, is well named. Built in 1593 in the reign of Elizabeth I, it was part of a much larger fortification called the Garrison.

The Garrison demonstrates the anxiety felt about invasion by Spain in the latter part of Elizabeth I's reign. The Isles of Scilly – a group of islands with safe anchorage off Land's End in Cornwall – were a good vantage point from which an approaching invasion fleet could be sighted, and building a fortress here was an important part of English defence planning.

LEFT: *Sudeley Castle, near Winchcombe in Gloucestershire, was a fortified manor house built on the site of a 12th-century castle in 1442. During the Civil War, it was held for Charles I by Lord Chandos, who although he later joined the Parliamentarians, could not prevent the castle being slighted. It was restored in the 19th century.*

ABOVE: *Crathes Castle, in Aberdeenshire, was built between 1553 and 1596, and combines the advantages of a fortified tower-house with an interesting domestic interior. As well as a noble hall on the first floor, there are well-preserved painted ceilings, and a long gallery, which runs across the building, and was used for exercise on wet days.*

LEFT: *Longford Castle, southeast of Salisbury, in Wiltshire, has the distinction of not having been destroyed by Oliver Cromwell's troops, although it was besieged during the Civil War. Built to an unusual triangular design in 1591, it originally had a matching triangular moat. The gardens were landscaped in the 18th and 19th centuries.*

ABOVE: *St Catherine's Castle, at Fowey on the coast of Cornwall, was built by Henry VIII in the 1520s. Although it resembles a medieval castle, it is in fact an artillery fort with wide gunports (six at floor level) and a much lower profile. Henry had a profound knowledge of artillery and was keen to apply it to the design of his coastal defences.*

A partially fortified and crenellated tower-house, built by William Ingilby in the mid-16th century, is visible in the present structure of Ripley Castle, in North Yorkshire. In the late 18th century, Ripley was enlarged by the addition of a country house built on the site of what had been a medieval hall adjacent to the tower.

With a turret at each corner, the uncompromisingly rectangular design of Lulworth
Castle, in Dorset, harks back to 12th-century military architecture, although the
building originated as an early 17th-century hunting lodge. It escaped serious
damage during the Civil War, unlike its near neighbour, Corfe Castle.

ABOVE: *Callaly Castle, in Northumberland, conceals its fortified origins – a massive 15th-century pele tower – within the structure of the large country house of which it now consists. A pele tower – common in the troubled Borders country – was essentially a fortified house, where animals could be herded, on the ground floor, while their owners took refuge on the upper floor.*

LEFT: *The history of Berwick-upon-Tweed, in Northumberland, reflects the struggle between Scotland and England over the border between the two countries. The magnificent walls and ramparts that surround the town date from the reign of Elizabeth I when Berwick finally came under English control in 1482.*

LEFT: *Basing House, near Basingstoke in Hampshire, was originally a motte-and-bailey castle. It was rebuilt as a vast crenellated palace by the Marquess of Winchester in 1535. The fifth Marquess, John Paulet, made Basing a centre for Royalist and Catholic sympathizers. It caught the attention of Cromwell's troops, who stormed it in 1645, causing great slaughter and the destruction of what had been the largest private house in the land.*

ABOVE: *The surrender of Raglan Castle, in Monmouthshire, after an 11-week siege by Parliamentarian forces in 1646, signalled the end of the stronghold. It belonged to the Earl of Worcester, a fanatical Royalist and reputedly the richest man in England. The once-magnificent castle suffered a daily bombardment of 60 shot, each of 18–20 lb (8–9 kg). The contents of the earl's library – a superb collection – were burnt by the Parliamentarians.*

ABOVE: *In the late 16th century, the medieval structure of Powis Castle, near Welshpool in Powys, was remodelled by its new owner, Edward Herbert. This restructuring formed part of the trend away from the draughty inconvenience of stone castles towards much greater domestic comfort. Herbert built the long gallery, an important feature of grand Tudor country houses.*

RIGHT: *Thornbury, in Gloucestershire, can be described as the last of the old-style English castles. Built by the Duke of Buckingham in 1511, it exemplifies the highly decorated defensible palace rather than the utilitarian fortress. It was confiscated by Henry VIII, and after the Civil War, it fell into disrepair, although it was restored in the 19th century.*

ABOVE: *The present structure of Sissinghurst Castle, in Kent, retains vestiges of its former glory. Built in the 16th century, on the site of a medieval moated manor farm as a grand Tudor courtyard house, it was replaced later in the century by a new mansion with a four-storey tower and two octagonal turrets. The tower now forms the focal point of the famous gardens.*

RIGHT: *Built in 1456, Knole House, near Sevenoaks in Kent, is a fine example of the architecture of the late Middle Ages. This was a time when castles were giving way to great country houses, homes for the rich and powerful. It passed into royal ownership in the reign of Henry VIII. His daughter, Elizabeth I, presented it to Thomas Sackville, her cousin. The house remained in the ownership of his descendants until 1946.*

THE ROMANTIC AGE

'The monstrous practice of castle building is, unhappily, not yet extinct … The largest and most carefully and learnedly executed Gothic mansion of the present day is a real and carefully constructed medieval fortress…. Now this is the very height of masquerading.'

SIR GEORGE GILBERT SCOTT, REMARKS ON SECULAR AND DOMESTIC ARCHITECTURE, 1857

By the mid–18th century, and for reasons ranging from domestic stability to the military concerns of a wider world, the age of the castle as a functioning, garrisoned fortress was over. Castles had virtually been consigned to history, but it was precisely at this time that romantic concepts of the age of chivalry, and of the castle, began to develop in Britain. Many historic castles underwent not only restoration but remodelling that reflected this new fashion for medievalism. On the practical side, this romantic revival, and the costly conversions that it demanded, was aided in no small part by material wealth, brought to the upper classes by a boom in the value of their assets, and to the middle classes by the Industrial Revolution and its legacy in the later 19th century. On the creative side it was the architect John Nash, and the landscape designers Humphry Repton and Capability Brown, that fulfilled the dreams of their patrons. Soon the stately, romantic castle took the form of comfortable residence, with the trappings of medieval fortifications, set in artfully contrived 'natural' surroundings. In Scotland, the cult of the romantic castle reached a particularly refined, even saccharine level.

ABOVE: *Picton Castle, just outside Haverfordwest in Pembrokeshire, originated as a simple earthwork fortification. A new stone castle was built nearby in about 1250, but this was dramatically altered in the 17th and 18th centuries, when Picton was transformed into a Georgian residence.*

LEFT: *Designed in 1910 by Edwin Lutyens for Julius Drewe, a retired businessman, the granite bulk of Castle Drogo, on the edge of Dartmoor, overlooks the beautiful valley of the River Teign.*

It is not entirely surprising that the castle should have been resurrected as an architectural style, as opposed to a military instrument. Indeed in some respects the idiom of castellation had never been abandoned, having been adopted as a mainly or even purely decorative feature quite early in the history of the medieval stone castle. Henry III put 'fake' battlements on some of his country houses and hunting-boxes. He thus inaugurated a habit of conscious antiquarianism, or pseudo-chivalry, which became a feature of genuine castles in the 15th century. The Tudors, although anxious to dissociate themselves from so many social and political aspects of the Middle Ages, were devoted to what they saw as romantic embellishments – pedigrees, coats-of-arms, joustings and mock-combats. It was inevitable that this kind of revivalism should also express itself in architecture.

The true medieval-romantic revival, however, did not take place until nearly 100 years later, when leading aesthetes and craftsmen began to react forcefully against the rigidity and symmetry of Classicism. Culzean Castle, as remodelled by Robert Adam, Vanbrugh Castle, and Walpole's Strawberry Hill were signs of the times. The first real centre of the cult was Herefordshire, already rich in ruinous castles of the Welsh Marches. One of them, Croft Castle, was owned by Richard Knight, the son of a wealthy iron-master from Shropshire, then in the first stages of the Industrial Revolution. The castle dated from the late 14th and early 15th centuries, and was large and quadrangular, with four round corner-towers. In the decade 1750–60, Knight 'gothicized' it, inside and out. His nephew, Richard Payne Knight, carried the process a stage further. In 1772–8 he built Downton Castle in the Herefordshire forest of Bringewood. Building the castle, on a magnificent site overlooking the River Teme with woody crags below, was an exercise in landscaping. It is one of the earliest contrived mansions in the castle style.

The great Humphry Repton published *Sketches and Hints on Landscape Gardening* in 1795. It was Repton's collaboration with the architect John Nash, who was taken up by the Prince Regent and many other wealthy amateurs, that really began the vogue of castle building. At Luscombe, in Devon, the banker Charles Hoare commissioned the pair to create for him a gothic castle and its setting. Here, the effect is not of weightiness, but of a delightful airiness and lightness, emphasized by the large, low, delicate gothic windows. But perhaps inevitably, and certainly in lesser hands, gothicization tended to produce the ponderous. At Eastnor, again in Herefordshire, Sir Robert Smirke built for the 2nd Lord Somers, from 1812, a gigantic replica of what he imagined a medieval castle should be.

Still further from the Nash-Repton mode was Penrhyn Castle, built for the Welsh slate-millionaire George Hay Dawkins-Pennant, from 1827 onwards. The home of the Tudor dynasty in the 14th century, Penrhyn had already been reconstructed as a 'medieval' house by Samuel Wyatt in 1782. But then, with the publication of Scott's *Ivanhoe* in 1820, came the 'Norman Revival', and Thomas Hopper was brought in to 'Normanize' the castle. The broad, high keep was square, sombre, and modelled on Rochester and Hedingham. There was a circular tower, a barbican, and defensible walls; even the drawing-room and the library were 'Norman', and remarkably well done too.

With Penrhyn, and other vast gothic piles put up at the same period, the impulse changed from the purely aesthetic to the historical and the quest for reproductive accuracy. Rich men began to want to relive medieval scenes against an appropriate architectural background. But was 'the real thing' desirable? Nash, for instance, had used a gothic vernacular, but he had not aimed to create authentic castles. But by the 1840s and 1850s that was precisely what architects and their patrons were doing. Sir George Gilbert Scott, the leading theorist, did not approve of the trend. Architecture, he felt, should reflect the nature of society: he feared that the cult of building castles, and imitation castles at that, not by nobility, but by men who had made their money in trade, threatened to bring into contempt and ridicule the concept of social order. Building an imitation castle, he felt, was an 'unreal task' with which to charge an architect.

Anthony Salvin, who created the extraordinary Peckforton Castle, in Cheshire, was perhaps the best, and purest, of the imitation-castle designers. He understood what medieval military engineering was about; but he was no head-in-the-air romantic. When the 1st Lord Tollemache decided to build at Peckforton in 1844, Salvin was recommended to him 'for the way in which he can combine the exterior and plan of an Edwardian castle with 19th-century elegance and comfort'. Peckforton has great medieval authenticity. Its towers are not too high for use, and it gives the impression of being defensible.

Other Victorian exercises in the castle-style survive, notably the two masterly reconstructions that William Burges created for the 3rd Marquess of Bute at Cardiff and Castell Coch. The Butes were a wealthy Scottish family, with extensive estates in Wales, who became multi-millionaires in the mid-19th century. The 3rd marquess was fascinated by the medieval past, and by the desire to re-create it. In 1865, he joined forces with Burges, who had noted the possibilities offered by the ruined Norman castle of Cardiff. Burges, like Bute, was a passionate medievalist. He was a skilled decorator as well as an architect, and his plans for Cardiff were both monumental and riotously elaborate. He worked there from 1868 until his death in 1881.

Of course Cardiff does not look like any medieval castle that ever existed. But at Castell Coch, also near Cardiff, on the site of an old motte-and-bailey castle that had been destroyed in the 15th century, Burges came much closer to the Salvin manner in the use of massive stonework. He followed the original ground plan, but his concept of the shape and height of the towers and curtain was purely conjectural. The courtyard, too, though immensely impressive in its massive strength, is unlike any medieval model anywhere. On the other hand, the well is genuine, there are proper 'murder holes' above the gateway, and the cellar-dungeon has an authentic look.

Meanwhile many of the stately castles of England were undergoing less imaginative but equally thoroughgoing restorations and transformations. Eaton Hall, Arundel and Belvoir are good examples, but these undertakings produced very mixed results. Dunster Castle, in Somerset, was splendidly remodelled: the result is one of the most attractive architectural medleys in Britain, though, apart from its foundations, it is essentially a Victorianized Elizabethan-Jacobean-Restoration manor house, rather than a medieval stronghold.

North of the border, the castle had never been abandoned as the customary habitation of the upper classes, but there, too, it enjoyed an architectural revival in the closing decades of the 18th century, just as the clan system was dissolving as a military force. At Inveraray the Dukes of Argyll completely reconstructed their early 16th-century castle, according to an eclectic château-plan. The result, completed in 1770, with its blue-green granite and Victorian green cone-towers, is a magnificent essay in castellated pastiche. A decade later, Robert Adam turned Culzean Castle, in Ayrshire, on its wild, cliff-top site, into a stately Georgian mansion with Gothic embellishments.

With the 19th century, and the commercial boom in the highland way of life, many great tower-house castles of the 15th, 16th and 17th centuries were expanded and modernized. Glamis was more than doubled in size, not really to the advantage of its appearance. At Dunrobin, on the coast of Sutherland, a modest medieval castle was transformed, in 1844–50, into a vast and highly decorative château,

Between 1808 and 1812 more than 100 Martello towers were built along England's southeastern coast to defend Britain against invasion by Napoleon. The northernmost, at Aldburgh, on the Suffolk coast, has a unique quatrefoil design but, like all the others, it was constructed as a self-contained gun tower capable of withstanding bombardment under siege.

with a silhouette of breathtaking extravagance. These are all matters of taste. So, too, are the brand new exercises in Scottish baronial that date from the middle years of the 19th century and later. At Balmoral, in 1848, Queen Victoria and Prince Albert, having bought a highland property they had never seen, arrived to find 'a pretty little castle in the old Scotch style'. In fact, it had been built less than 20 years before. Later, the royal couple demolished the 'pretty little castle', and built Balmoral, believed to be the largest castle in Scotland. The architect was William Smith but he merely looked after the details: the castle was, as the queen said: 'My dearest Albert's own creation, own work, own building, own laying out.' The great square tower is 80 ft (24 m) high, which to some may seem top-heavy, and the interior incorporates a huge ballroom and ample drawing room.

Balmoral has had its critics. Its decorations were described as 'tartanities'. Lord Clarendon thought the plaids there 'would rejoice the heart of a donkey'; the whole place he summed up as 'the scramble of rural royalty'. But others, beside Queen Victoria, liked Balmoral, and still do. For it, and its many imitations, seemed to sum up the spirit and aspirations of those who refuse, even today, to believe that the age of the castle is entirely dead, and who still try to prolong it into an alien and mundane epoch.

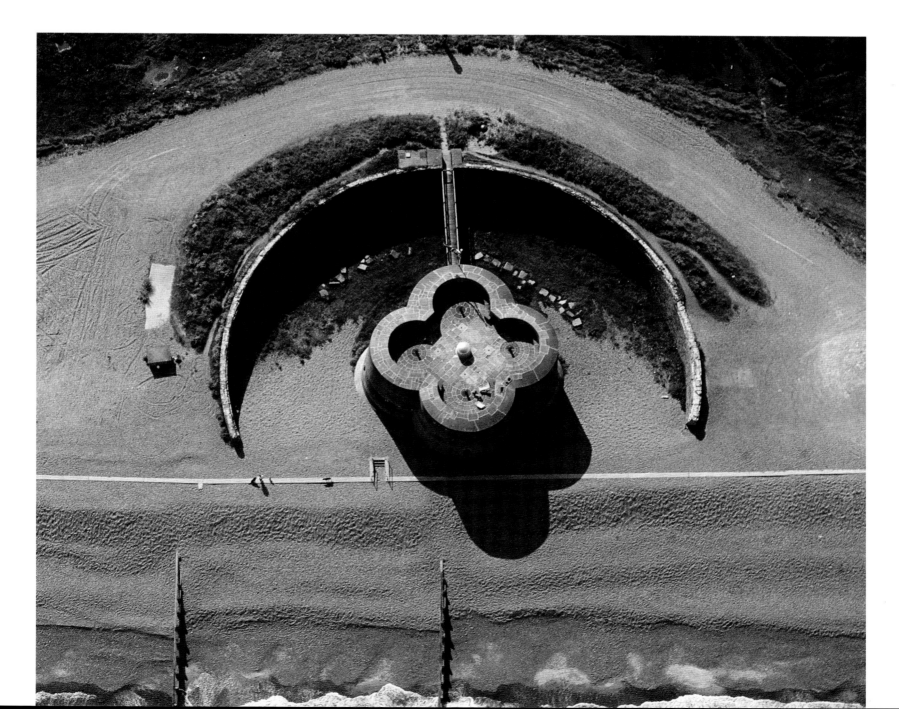

LEFT: *Eastnor Castle, in Herefordshire, was built in the early 19th century as a re-creation of a Norman stronghold. Designed by the architect Robert Smirke for the first Earl Somers, the building took ten years to construct. In 1849, the architect Augustus Pugin, was invited to decorate the drawing room.*

ABOVE: *Until 1976, Dunster Castle – on the edge of Exmoor, near the coast of North Somerset – had been the home of the Luttrell family for 600 years. The medieval fortress has all but disappeared in the extensive rebuilding that took place in the 17th and 19th centuries, most notably when the architect Anthony Salvin remodelled the castle between 1868 and 1872.*

LEFT: *Just across the valley from the medieval ruins of Beeston Castle, in Cheshire, lies Peckforton – the Victorian re-creation of a Norman fortress. Now a luxury hotel, Peckforton was designed by Anthony Salvin for John Tollemache, who represented Cheshire in parliament for more than 30 years in the 19th century.*

ABOVE: *The present imposing structure of Lambton Castle, situated in the coal-mining area of northeast England, near Washington in County Durham, is mostly the creation of John Lambton, the first Earl of Durham, at the beginning of the 19th century. The Italian-born Joseph Bonomi and his son, Ignatius, were commissioned as architects.*

ABOVE: *Alton Castle, east of Stoke-on-Trent, in Staffordshire, is probably at least the third fortification to be built on the site over the past 900 years. It was constructed to a design by Augustus Pugin (who also worked on the Houses of Parliament), who was commissioned by the 16th Earl of Shrewsbury in 1837.*

RIGHT: *The architect Charles Barry, who collaborated with Augustus Pugin on the design for the Houses of Parliament, was largely responsible for the creation of Highclere Castle. Located south of Newbury, in Berkshire, Highclere is the seat of the Earls of Caernarvon. The building's construction and the decoration of the interior took more than 30 years to complete.*

BRITISH ISLES
INVADERS AND SETTLERS
AD 43–1588

This image shows the routes taken by the main raiders, invaders and settlers over 1,500 years from the coming of the Romans to the time of the Spanish Armada. Please note that this is a satellite photograph to show the geographical context for the British Isles and not a map giving precise routes.

Vikings from Norway

Shetland Isles •
Viking settlement
c. AD 700

Orkney
Islands
Viking
settlement
c. AD 800

NORWAY

Hebrides

SCOTLAND

NORTH
SEA

Iona •
Vikings attacked
AD 795

Edinburgh •

NORTH
ATLANTIC

• Lindisfarne
Vikings attacked
AD 793

Hadrian's
Wall

Vikings from Denmark
9th century AD

• York
ruled by
Vikings
from AD 866

Angles
from c. AD 450

IRELAND

Dublin
Viking
occupation
AD 839 •

Anglesey

Saxons
from c. AD 450

Offa's
Dyke

ENGLAND

WALES

Jutes from
c. AD 450

• Cardiff

London •

Richborough
Dover •
Lympne •

Gravelines

Pevensey •

Scilly
Isles

ENGLISH
CHANNEL

Normans
1066

Romans
AD 43

Boulogne

• Dieppe

• Caen

Normandy

Brittany

LIST OF MONARCHS FROM 1066

William I	1066–87	Henry VI	1422–61 and 1470–71 (deposed by Edward IV, murdered in May 1471)	James II	1685–88
William II	1087–1100			William and Mary	1689–1702
Henry I	1100–35	Edward IV	1461–70 and 1471–83	Anne	1702–14
Stephen	1135–54	Edward V	1483	George I	1714–27
Henry II	1154–89	Richard III	1483–85	George II	1727–60
Richard I	1189–99	Henry VII	1485–1509	George III	1760–1820
John	1199–1216	Henry VIII	1509–47	George IV	1820–30
Henry III	1216–72	Edward VI	1547–53	William IV	1830–37
Edward I	1272–1307	Jane	1553 (executed in 1554)	Victoria	1837–1901
Edward II	1307–27	Mary I	1553–58	Edward VII	1901–10
Edward III	1327–77	Elizabeth I	1558–1603	George V	1910–36
Richard II	1377–99	James I	1603–25	Edward VIII	1936 (abdicated)
Henry IV	1399–1413	Charles I	1625–49 (executed January 1649)	George VI	1936–52
Henry V	1413–22	Charles II	1660–85	Elizabeth II	1952–present

TIMELINE FROM ROMAN INVASION OF BRITAIN TO RESTORATION OF MONARCHY

AD **43** More than 40,000 troops land on Kent coast – beginning of the Roman conquest of what is to become the province of Britannia. Iron Age tribes are overcome by superior Roman military strength, either destroyed or assimilated into the Roman way of life.

AD **61** Revolt by Boudicca, widow of the leader of the Iceni tribe, against Roman rule. St Albans and London are destroyed by the rebels and their populations massacred. Boudicca and her forces eventually defeated by Roman troops.

121–126 Construction of Hadrian's Wall.

c.410 Withdrawal of Roman legions and gradual collapse of Romano-British society.

c.450 Settlement by Germanic peoples begins – including Angles, Saxons and Jutes.

597 Monk named Augustine lands in Kent to begin conversion of England to Christianity. Augustine appointed first Archbishop of Canterbury.

793 Norse raiders attack and burn monastery of Lindisfarne, an early documented example of a Viking raid on Britain.

c.860 The beginning of Viking settlement in large parts of northern and eastern England.

878 The Saxon King Alfred builds fort at Athelney in Somerset – the start of the refortification of England against Viking raiders.

1066 Battle of Hastings. Invasion force led by William of Normandy defeats army of English King Harold. William crowned king on Christmas Day. Almost immediately, Normans begin to build castles across the country.

c.1090 Norman Conquest extended into Wales and Scotland.

1095 Pope Urban II gives speech urging knights of Europe to recover Jerusalem from the control of Seljuk Turks. The First Crusade sets out the following year.

1135–54 Civil war in England – a struggle for the throne of England – between King Stephen and Matilda, daughter of Henry I. Many unlicensed castles built, which Henry II later destroys.

1215 The unpopular King John signs the Magna Carta – the Great Charter – an agreement between the king and his barons that curbs the power of the sovereign.

1277 Edward I begins extensive castle-building programme in Wales with innovations in design, part of his campaign to subdue the Welsh.

1281 Edward I grants licence to Lawrence of Ludlow, permitting him to build an early surviving example of a fortified manor house – Stokesay Castle, in Shropshire.

1301 Edward I creates his son (later Edward II) Prince of Wales.

1314 Edward II defeated by Robert the Bruce at Bannockburn.

c.1326 Introduction of first cannon using gunpowder.

1349 First outbreak of what later became known as the 'Black Death' killing about a third of the population in England. The labour shortage in the following years, means that the king is able to 'impress' or force masons and carpenters to work on castle building.

1370s Edward III loses command of the sea. English coasts – especially the southeast – now open to attack from France and her ally, Spain. Many town walls, such as Canterbury, were strengthened. In especially vulnerable areas, a number of castles were built and manor houses were fortified.

1381 Peasants' Revolt – a rebellion against the feudal system. Feudalism meant that the Church and landowners had the legal right to force their estate workers to give labour free of charge. The death of the rebel leader, Wat Tyler, and assurances given by the king, Richard II, (which were never fulfilled) spelled the end of the revolt.

1405 Developments in artillery demand changes in castle design. Cannons were now powerful enough to win sieges such as those at the castles of Alnwick, Berwick and Warkworth.

1455 Beginning of the Wars of the Roses, a series of English civil wars lasting 32 years and arising largely from rival claims to the throne by two dynasties – the house of York and the house of Lancaster.

1485 Battle of Bosworth Field when Henry Tudor fights Richard III – the last Plantagenet king – for the crown of England. Richard is killed and his army defeated. Henry's coronation as Henry VII marks the beginning of the Tudor dynasty.

1529 Henry VIII seeks divorce from his first wife, Catherine of Aragon. The pope refuses to grant Henry a divorce, setting in motion a series of events leading ultimately to England leaving the Roman Catholic Church and becoming a Protestant country, with the sovereign and not the pope as the head of the Church.

1536 Act of Union joining Wales and England.

1588 Large fleet of Spanish ships sets sail, part of an attempt to invade England and overthrow Elizabeth I. The attempt fails, partly because of storms and partly because of attacks by English fleets.

1603 James VI of Scotland becomes James I of England on death of Elizabeth I, the beginning of the Stuart dynasty.

1605 A plot by Roman Catholics to blow up the Houses of Parliament killing the king is thwarted when Guy Fawkes is arrested and the explosives are discovered in a cellar under the House of Lords.

1628 Charles I dissolves Parliament, part of a long-running dispute between the Stuart kings and parliament, which is not recalled for 11 years.

1640 Charles I recalls Parliament to request money from tax revenue to put down a rebellion in Scotland. This parliament lasts three weeks, but Charles is forced to summon it again a month later after a Scottish invasion of England. This time it lasts until 1660, and is successful in achieving a measure of constitutional reform, although it highlights the differences between the reformers and the more conservative elements supporting the king.

1642 Beginning of the English Civil War between forces loyal to the Crown (known as Cavaliers or Royalists) and those who want reform of the constitution (Roundheads or Parliamentarians).

1645 Battle of Naseby – an important battle of the war – where Parliamentary forces under the command of Oliver Cromwell defeat Royalists. Charles I forced to retreat.

1649 Execution of Charles I. The monarchy is abolished, and during an 11-year period known generally as 'The Commonwealth', England is ruled first by Parliament, then by Oliver Cromwell as Lord Protector. Cromwell's son, Richard, briefly succeeds him but, in 1659, Parliament invites the exiled eldest son of Charles I to return to England.

1660 Monarchy restored under Charles II.

GLOSSARY OF TECHNICAL TERMS

Angevin: a member of the royal house of Anjou descended from Geoffrey of Anjou, especially the Plantagenet dynasty that ruled England from 1154 to 1216.

Angles, Saxons and Jutes: Germanic tribes who migrated to Britain in the 5th century after the departure of the Romans.

Anglo-Saxons: first used to differentiate between English Saxons and those in mainland Europe; later used to describe the pre-Norman, non-Celtic population of England.

Arbalaster: crossbowman.

Ashlar: worked stone with flat surface, usually of regular shape and with square edges.

Bailey: castle courtyard and surrounding buildings enclosed by a wall or palisade. *See Motte-and-bailey castle.*

Ballista: military machine similar to a large crossbow and capable of hurling javelins or rocks.

Barbican: outwork defending the gateway or entrance to a castle.

Bartizan: overhanging corner turret, battlemented and corbelled out; common in Scotland (and France).

Bastion: any fortified place; or solid masonry projection in a fortification designed to allow the face of a castle wall to be covered by fire.

Batter: inclined face of wall; hence battered.

Battlements: parapet with indentations or embrasures, with raised portions (merlons) between; also called crenellations.

Bayeux Tapestry: an embroidered cloth more than 200 ft (60 m) long, dating probably from the late 11th century, depicting the story of the Norman invasion of England. The tapestry is an important source of information on weapons and warfare of the period, and also includes an image of a motte castle being built at Hastings after the Normans landed.

Bede: Venerable Bede, Northumbrian monk and historian (AD 672/3–735), and author of *Ecclesiastical History of the English People.*

Belgae: Tribe from present area of northeastern France and the low countries, some of whom migrated into southern Britain around the 1st century BC.

Berm: level area, especially outside a hillfort, separating a ditch from a bank.

Bivalate: a hillfort defended by two concentric ditches.

Boss: central stone of an arch or vault, often decorated or painted.

Bratice: timber tower, or projecting wooden gallery.

Bronze Age: period of prehistory, in Britain c.1800 to 600 BC.

Buttress: a construction built to support a wall.

Castellan: officer in charge of a castle.

Cistercian: a monastic order responsible for the construction of many abbeys in Britain.

Cob: unburnt clay mixed with straw.

Concentric castle: castle with one or more rings of defensive walls.

Constable: official in charge of a castle in its owner's absence.

Corbel: projecting stone.

Counterscarp: outer slope of ditch.

Crenel: gap in battlemented parapet; crenellate: to fortify.

Crossbow: weapon for firing bolts (also known as quarrels) using a mechanism to wind and shoot the bolts. Often made of maple or oak.

Crosswall: interior dividing wall of castle.

Curtain: connecting wall 'hung' between the towers of a castle.

Dark Ages: period of British history between the departure of the Romans in the 5th century AD and about AD 1000. Described as 'Dark' since few records of the periods survive.

Donjon: Norman-French word for principal tower or keep of a castle, from which the English word 'dungeon' is derived.

Drawbridge: movable bridge; originally moved horizontally like a gangway.

Dressing: carved stonework around openings.

Drum-towers: large, circular towers, usually low and squat.

Drystone: unmortared masonry.

Durotriges: one of the tribes in Britain at time of Roman conquest, inhabiting an area roughly equivalent to modern Dorset.

Embattled: battlemented.

Embrasure: small opening in fortified parapet, usually splayed on inside.

Footings: bottom part of wall, including the foundations.

Forebuilding: block in front of keep, to form lobby or landing.

Fosse: ditch.

Franks: Tribal people who migrated into area covered by most of modern France and Franconia in Germany and established a powerful state here.

Gallery: long passage or room.

Garderobe: latrine; privy.

Great chamber: lord's solar, or bed-sitting room.

Greek fire: incendiary weapon used by Byzantine armies that ignited when exposed to water.

Hall: principal room or building in complex.

Hillfort: Bronze or Iron Age earthwork of ditches and banks.

Hoarding: Wooden structure temporarily built over castle walls for hurling missiles at attackers.

Invest: to surround a castle in preparation for a siege.

Iron Age: period of prehistory, in Britain from c.600 BC to the beginning of the Roman period c.50 BC.

John of Salisbury: Historian and monk (c.1115–80), and a witness to murder of Thomas Becket, Archbishop of Canterbury; his letters form an important historical source for period.

Keep: main tower of castle.

Lancet: long, narrow window with pointed head.

Light: component part of window, divided by mullions and transoms.

Lintel: horizontal stone or beam bridging an opening such as a door or window.

Longbow: English longbow, also known as the Welsh longbow, a powerful type of bow, up to 6 ft (2 m) long, made of elm, yew or boxwood, with a long range, held and fired in vertical position. Used by English archers at the Battle of Agincourt.

Loop: narrow opening in a defensive wall.

Machicolation: projecting gallery on brackets, on outside of castle tower or walls, with holes in floor through which missiles could be dropped on assailants.

Mangonel: siege engine whose projectile arms turn against fixed stop.

Merlon: solid part of embattled parapet.

Meurtrière: an opening in roof of passage through which missiles could be shot down on to attackers below.

Milecastle: fortified gateways or fortlets built at intervals of one Roman mile along the length of Hadrian's Wall.

Mine gallery: siege work to cause wall-collapse.

Moat: deep defensive ditch encircling a fortification filled with water.

Motte: a natural or man-made mound, on which a keep was built, particularly in the 11th and 12th centuries. *See Motte-and-bailey castle.*

Motte-and-bailey castle: fortification consisting of a wooden or stone keep surrounded by a ditched and palisaded enclosure or courtyard.

Multivallate: hillfort with three or more concentric lines of defence.

Norman: person from Normandy, area in northern France settled by Vikings in the 10th century AD.

Norse: people originating from Scandinavia.

Palisade: timber defensive screen or fence.

Parapet: low wall on outer side of main wall.

Pele tower: type of fortified tower-house, able to withstand short siege, built in border area between England and Scotland in the 13th and 14th centuries.

Picts: inhabitants of northern Scotland in Roman times.

Plantagenet: Another name for Angevin kings of England. *See Angevin.*

Plinth: projecting base of wall.

Portcullis: grating dropped vertically from grooves to block passage or gate in castle; of wood, metal or a combination of the two.

Postern: back door of castle.

Quadrangle: inner courtyard.

Quatrefoil: design with four lobes.

Rampart: defensive stone or earth wall surrounding castle or town.

Ravelin: outwork with two faces forming a salient angle.

Ring-work: circular earthwork of bank and ditch.

Romanesque: prevailing architectural style, 8th to 12th century, with rounded arches.

Rubble: unsquared stone not laid in courses.

Scarp: slope on inner side of ditch.

Shell keep: circular or oval wall surrounding inner portion of castle.

Siege tower: tall wooden tower used by besiegers to gain access to the top of castle walls.

Slight: partial or total destruction of a castle to render it unusable for future defensive or offensive purposes. Particularly practised during the English Civil War in the 1640s by Parliamentary troops.

Solar: upper living room of a medieval house or castle; often over the hall.

Squint: observation hole in wall or room.

Stone Age: period in prehistoric Britain when tools were manufactured from stone, extending from time of first human settlement up to the beginning of metalworking around 1800 BC.

Trebuchet: siege engine with unequal counterpoise arm.

Trefoil: three-lobed.

Turret: small tower, round or polygonal.

Vault: stone roofing.

Vikings: Norse raiders from Scandinavia.

Voussoir: wedge-shaped stone in arch.

Wall-stair: staircase built into thickness of wall.

Wall walk: passage along castle wall.

Ward: courtyard or bailey of castle.

Weathering: sloping surface to throw off rainwater.

William of Malmesbury: monk and historian, c.1090–1143. Important source for history of early Norman kings.

William of Newburgh: historian and canon of Newburgh Priory, Yorkshire, 1136–98, important historical source, especially for Henry II.

Wing-wall: wall down slope of motte to protect stairway.

Yett: iron gate.

GAZETTEER

Britain has an exceptionally rich heritage of hillforts, castles and fortified houses that reflect historical changes spanning some 2,000 years. Some places have survived and are still occupied as family homes, occasionally by descendants of the people who first built them. The remains of others are more fragmentary, but stone castles were built to endure and many of them have done just that, and are often in an extremely good state of preservation. Visitors are welcomed at many of these historic places. Some sites are privately owned, while others are in the care of local authorities. Many in England and Wales are owned or managed by The National Trust; similarly many sites in Scotland are owned or managed by The National Trust for Scotland. There are government agencies with special responsibilities to protect and promote Britain's ancient buildings and sites – Cadw in Wales, English Heritage and Historic Scotland. Contact details for these heritage bodies, including websites, are listed on page 216. (Numbers in brackets after a castle's name indicate the page on which a photograph appears.)

Abbotsbury	South-West England
Aberdour	Scotland
Abergavenny	Wales
Aberlleiniog	Wales
Abernathy	Scotland
Aberrheidol	Wales
Aberystwyth (and Pen Dinas Iron Age Fort) *(132)*	Wales
Ackergill Tower	Scotland
Acton Burnell	Welsh Marches
Affleck	Scotland
Airth	Scotland
Aldeburgh *(201)*	Eastern England
Allington *(111)*	London & South-East England
Alnwick *(52–3)*	North-East England
Alton *(206)*	Central England
Amberley	London & South-East England
Amhuinnsuidhe	Scotland
Amroth	Wales
Ancaster	Eastern England
Antonine Wall	Scotland
Anwoth	Scotland
Appleby	North-West England
Arbeia	North-East England
Ardestie	Scotland
Ardoch	Scotland
Ardtornish	Scotland
Ardunie	Scotland
Ardverikie	Scotland
Ardvourlie	Scotland
Ardvreck	Scotland
Arka-Unskel	Scotland
Armadale	Scotland
Arnot Tower	Scotland
Aros	Scotland
Arundel *(2; 54–5)*	London & South-East England
Ascot D'Oyly	London & South-East England
Ashby de la Zouch	Central England
Auchen	Scotland
Auchindoun	Scotland
Aydon	North-East England
Ayton	North-East England
Baconsthorpe	Eastern England
Badbury Rings *(9)*	South-West England
Baldoon	Scotland
Balfour	Scotland
Balgonie	Scotland
Balhousie	Scotland
Ballencrieff	Scotland
Ballinbreich	Scotland
Ballindalloch	Scotland
Balmoral	Scotland
Baltersan	Scotland
Balvaird	Scotland
Balvenie	Scotland
Bamburgh *(38–9; 94–5)*	North-East England
Bar Hill	Scotland
Barcaldine	Scotland
Barden Tower *(154)*	North-East England
Barholm	Scotland
Barnard Castle *(90–91)*	North-East England
Barnwell	Central England
Barr	Scotland
Barryhill (or Barra Hill)	Scotland
Basing House *(192)*	London & South-East England
Battlesbury Camp Hillfort *(28)*	South-West England
Bayard's Cove Fort	South-West England
Beacon Hillfort *(32–3)*	London & South East England
Beadnell Tower	North-East England
Bearsden	Scotland
Beaumaris *(116–17)*	Wales
Bedford	Eastern England
Bedlay	Scotland
Beeston *(84–5)*	Welsh Marches
Belsay	North-East England
Belvoir	Central England
Benton	Wales
Berkeley *(98)*	South-West England
Berkhamsted	Eastern England
Berry Pomeroy	South-West England
Berwick-upon-Tweed (Castle and Walls) *(190–91)*	North-East England
Beverston	Welsh Marches
Bickleigh	South-West England
Bindon Hill	South-West England
Birdoswald	North-East England
Birrens	Scotland
Birse	Scotland
Blackbury	South-West England
Blackcraig	Scotland
Blackness	Scotland
Blaenllynfi	Wales
Blair	Scotland
Blairquhan	Scotland
Blervie	Scotland
Bodiam *(126–7)*	London & South-East England
Bolingbroke	Eastern England
Bolsover *(178–9)*	Central England
Bolton *(102)*	North-East England
Borthwick	Scotland
Bothal	North-East England
Bothwell	Scotland
Bowes	North-East England
Bowness on Solway	North-West England
Braemar	Scotland
Brahan	Scotland
Bramber	London & South-East England
Brancaster	Eastern England
Brancepeth	North-East England
Brandon Camp	Welsh Marches
Branxholme	Scotland
Bratton Camp *(12)*	South-West England
Brecon (Castle and Town)	Wales
Brecon Gaer	Wales
Breidden (or Breiddin) Hillfort	Wales
Brent Knoll	South-West England
Brims	Scotland
Brinklow	Central England
Broch of Gurness *(18–19)*	Scotland
Broch of Midhowe	Scotland
Brodick	Scotland
Brodie	Scotland
Broncroft	Central England
Bronllys	Wales
Broomhall	Scotland
Brough	North-West England
Brougham (Castle and Hall)	North-West England
Broughton	Central England
Broughty	Scotland
Brown Cathertun	Scotland
Buchanan	Scotland
Buckland Rings Hillfort	London & South-East England
Builth	Wales
Bull Sand Fort (Humber Estuary)	North-East England
Bungay	Eastern England
Burgh (Castle and Gariannonum)	Eastern England
Burghead	Scotland
Burgi Geos	Scotland
Burleigh	Scotland
Burnswark Hill	Scotland
Burnt Island	Scotland
Burrough Hillfort	Central England
Burton Agnes	North-East England
Bury Hill	London & South-East England
Bury St Edmonds (Abbey Great Gate & St James' Tower)	Eastern England
Bute-Dunagoil	Scotland
Bywell	North-East England
Cadbury *(36)*	South-West England
Cadzow	Scotland
Caer Bran	South-West England
Caer Caradoc Hillfort	Wales
Caer Drewyn Hillfort	Wales
Caer Euni Hillfort	Wales
Caer Penrhos	Wales
Caergwrle *(see Hope)*	
Caerlaverock *(118)*	Scotland
Caerleon (Castle and Town)	Wales
Caernarfon (Castle and Town) *(152–3)*	Wales
Caernarfon (Segontium)	Wales
Caerphilly *(106–07)*	Wales
Caerwent (Castle and Town)	Wales
Caisteal Maol	Scotland
Caister	Eastern England
Caldicot *(144–5)*	Wales
Calgary	Scotland
Callaly *(191)*	North-East England
Calshot	London & South-East England
Caludon	Central England
Camber *(1; 169)*	London & South-East England
Cambridge	Eastern England
Campbell	Scotland
Canterbury (Castle and Walls) *(26)*	London & South-East England
Caprington	Scotland
Carbisdale	Scotland
Cardiff (Roman Fort and Castle) *(82)*	Wales
Cardigan	Wales
Cardoness	Scotland
Carew *(58–9; 138)*	Wales
Carisbrooke *(41; 174)*	London & South-East England
Carlisle *(94)*	North-West England
Carlungie	Scotland
Carmarthen	Wales
Carn Fadryn	Wales
Carn Goch Hillfort	Wales
Carn Liath	Scotland
Carn Nwchwn	Wales
Carnasserie	Scotland
Carnell	Scotland
Carrawburgh	North-East England
Carreg Cennen *(159)*	Wales
Carrick	Scotland
Carsluith	Scotland
Cary	Scotland
Castell Carndochan	Wales
Castell Coch	Wales
Castell-y-Bere *(82–3)*	Wales
Castle Acre *(68)*	Eastern England
Castle Bolton	North-East England
Castle Cornet (St Peter Port)	South-West England
Castle Craig	Scotland
Castle Dore	South-West England
Castle Drogo *(198–9)*	South-West England
Castle Elizabeth (St Helier)	South-West England
Castle Hill *(97)*	London & South-East England
Castle Howard	North-East England
Castle Kennedy	Scotland
Castle Lachlan	Scotland
Castle Leod	Scotland
Castle Levan	Scotland
Castle Menzies	Scotland
Castle Point	Scotland

Castle Rising (46)	Eastern England
Castle Rushen (Isle of Man)	North-West England
Castle Stalker	Scotland
Castle Stuart	Scotland
Castle Sween	Scotland
Castle Tioram	Scotland
Castle-an-Dinas (nr Penrith)	South-West England
Castle-an-Dinas (nr St Colomb Major)	South-West England
Castlelaw (and Castle Knowe)	Scotland
Cauadale	Scotland
Cawdor	Scotland
Cessnock	Scotland
Chepstow (Castle and Town) (92)	Wales
Chester (Castle and City Walls)	Welsh Marches
Chesterholm (see Vindolanda)	
Chesters (25)	North-East England
Chesters, The	Scotland
Chichester (Dykes and Walls)	London & South-East England
Chiddingstone	London & South-East England
Chilham (Castle and Manor House)	London & South-East England
Chillingham	North-East England
Chirk (139)	Wales
Christchurch	London & South-East England
Chun (10)	South-West England
Cil Ifor Top Hillfort (Gower)	Wales
Cilgerran	Wales
Cissbury Ring	London & South-East England
Clare	Eastern England
Clarghyll Hall Bastle Houses	North-West England
Claypotts	Scotland
Cley Hillfort (17)	South-West England
Clickhimin	Scotland
Clifford	Welsh Marches
Clitheroe	North-West England
Clovelly Dykes	South-West England
Clun	Welsh Marches
Coalhouse Fort (Tilbury)	Eastern England
Cocklaw Tower	North-East England
Codnor	Central England
Coity (70)	Wales
Colchester (Castle and Walls) (40)	Eastern England
Collairnie	Scotland
Comlongon	Scotland
Compton	South-West England
Compton Wynyates (152–3)	Central England
Conisbrough (63)	North-East England
Conwy (Castle and Town) (151)	Wales
Cooling	London & South-East England
Corbridge (Corstopitum)	North-East England
Corby	North-West England
Corfe (176–7)	South-West England
Corgarff	Scotland
Corsehope Rings	Scotland
Couston	Scotland
Cowdenknowes	Scotland
Craig Phadraig	Scotland
Craigend	Scotland
Craighall	Scotland
Craigievar	Scotland
Craigmillar	Scotland
Craignethan	Scotland
Craignish	Scotland
Craigston	Scotland
Cramond	Scotland
Craster Tower	North-East England
Crathes (185)	Scotland
Craufurdland	Scotland
Crayke	North-East England
Cresswell	North-East England
Criccieth (84)	Wales
Crichton	Scotland
Crickhowell	Wales
Cricklade	Welsh Marches
Croft	Welsh Marches
Cromarty	Scotland
Cromwell's Castle (Isles of Scilly)	South-West England
Crownhill Fort (Plymouth)	South-West England
Croy Hill	Scotland
Crug Hywel	Wales
Culcreuch	Scotland
Culsh	Scotland
Culzean	Scotland
Cwm Prysor	Wales
Dacre	North-West England
Dairsie	Scotland
Dalcross	Scotland
Dale Fort (Milford Haven)	Wales
Dalhousie	Scotland
Dalkeith	Scotland
Dalmahoy	Scotland
Dalnaglar	Scotland
Dalton	North-West England
Danebury Ring (31)	London & South-East England
Dartmouth	South-West England
Deal (162–3)	London & South-East England
Dean	Scotland
Deddington	Central England
Degannwy	Wales
Delgatie	Scotland
Denbigh (Castle and Town) (114)	Wales
Denmylne Tower	Scotland
Dere Street	Scotland
Deudraeth	Wales
Devil's Ditch	Eastern England
Devizes	South-West England
Din Eidyn	Scotland
Dinas Bran (or Castell Dinas) (28–9)	Wales
Dinas Emrys	Wales
Dinas Powys	Wales
Dinefwr (or Dynevor)	Wales
Dirleton	Scotland
Dod Law Hillfort	North-East England
Dolbadarn	Wales
Dolwyddelan	Wales
Donnington	London & South-East England
Doon Hill	Scotland
Dorchester	South-West England
Dornoch	Scotland
Douglas	Scotland
Doune (135)	Scotland
Dover (66–7)	London & South-East England
Downton	Welsh Marches
Dreva Craig	Scotland
Drum	Scotland
Drumin	Scotland
Drumlanrig	Scotland
Drummond	Scotland
Drumtochty	Scotland
Dryslwyn	Wales
Duart	Scotland
Duchal	Scotland
Dudhope	Scotland
Dudley	Central England
Duff House	Scotland
Duffield	Central England
Duffus	Scotland
Dumbarton	Scotland
Dumbarton Rock	Scotland
Dun Carloway	Scotland
Dun Craich	Scotland
Dun Dhardhail (Dunjardil)	Scotland
Dun Dornaigil	Scotland
Dun Gall	Scotland
Dun Ladaigh	Scotland
Dun Mac Sniachan (or Mac Uisneachain, or Macsnoichan)	Scotland
Dun Mac Tjisneachain	Scotland
Dun Telve	Scotland
Dun Troddan	Scotland
Dun Vulan	Scotland
Dunadd	Scotland
Dunbar	Scotland
Dunbeath	Scotland
Dundas	Scotland
Dunderave	Scotland
Dundonald	Scotland
Dundurn	Scotland
Dunnideer	Scotland
Dunnottar	Scotland
Dunollie	Scotland
Dunrobin	Scotland
Duns	Scotland
Dunscaith	Scotland
Dunstaffnage	Scotland
Dunstanburgh (110–11)	North-East England
Dunster (203)	South-West England
Duntrune	Scotland
Duntulm	Scotland
Dunure	Scotland
Dunvegan	Scotland
Dunyvaig	Scotland
Dupplin	Scotland
Durham (49)	North-East England
Durisdeer	Scotland
Dynevor (see Dinefwr)	
Earlshall	Scotland
East Cowes	London & South-East England
Eastbourne (Redoubt)	London & South-East England
Eastnor (202)	Welsh Marches
Eden	Scotland
Edinburgh (50–51)	Scotland
Edin's Hall	Scotland
Edlingham	North-East England
Edzell	Scotland
Eggardon Hillfort (16)	South-West England
Egremont	North-West England
Eildon Hill North	Scotland
Eilean Domhnuill	Scotland
Eilean Donan (6; 142)	Scotland
Eilean na Goar	Scotland
Elcho	Scotland
Elmley	Welsh Marches
Elsdon	North-East England
Eltham Palace	London & South-East England
Elton Hall (155)	Eastern England
Embleton Tower	North-East England
Erchless	Scotland
Esselmont, Castle of	Scotland
Etal	North-East England
Ethie	Scotland
Ewloe	Wales
Exeter (City Walls)	South-West England
Exeter (Rougemont Castle)	South-West England
Eynsford	London & South-East England
Falkland Palace	Scotland
Farleigh Hungerford (149)	South-West England
Farne Island Tower	North-East England
Farnham (87)	London & South-East England
Fasque	Scotland
Featherstone	North-East England
Fenton Tower	Scotland
Fernie	Scotland
Ferniehurst	Scotland
Ffridd Faldwyn	Wales
Figsbury Ring (30)	South-West England
Findlater	Scotland
Finhaven	Scotland
Flamborough	North-East England
Flint (112)	Wales
Floors	Scotland
Foel Trigarn (Foel Drygarn)	Wales
Fonmon	Wales
Forbes	Scotland
Ford	North-East England
Fordyce	Scotland
Fort Albert (Alderney)	South-West England
Fort Amherst (Chatham)	London & South-East England
Fort Blockhouse (Gosport)	London & South-East England
Fort Bourgoyne (Dover)	London & South-East England
Fort Brockhurst (Gosport)	London & South-East England
Fort Clarence (Rochester)	London & South-East England
Fort Clonque (Alderney)	South-West England
Fort Corblets (Alderney)	South-West England
Fort Cumberland (Portsea)	London & South-East England
Fort Darnet (Medway)	London & South-East England
Fort Doyle (Alderney)	South-West England
Fort Doyle (Guernsey)	South-West England
Fort George (nr Inverness)	Scotland
Fort Gilkicker (Gosport)	London & South-East England
Fort Grange (Gosport)	London & South-East England
Fort Grosnez (Alderney)	South-West England
Fort Horstead (Chatham)	London & South-East England
Fort Luton (Chatham)	London & South-East England
Fort Monckton (Gosport)	London & South-East England
Fort Nelson (Portsdown Hill behind Portsmouth)	London & South-East England
Fort Paull (nr Hull)	North-East England
Fort Pezeries (Guernsey)	South-West England
Fort Purbrook (Portsdown Hill behind Portsmouth)	London & South-East England
Fort Regent (St. Helier)	South-West England
Fort Rowner (Gosport)	London & South-East England
Fort Saumarez (Guernsey)	South-West England
Fort Southwick (Portsdown Hill behind Portsmouth)	London & South-East England
Fort Tourgis (Alderney)	South-West England
Fort Victoria (nr Yarmouth)	London & South-East England
Fort Widley (Portsdown Hill behind Portsmouth)	London & South-East England
Forter	Scotland
Fotheringay	Central England
Fouldry (see Piel)	
Foulis	Scotland
Framlingham (65)	Eastern England
Fraser	Scotland
Fulton Tower	Scotland
Fyvie	Scotland

Pembroke (Castle and Town) (60–61) — Wales
Pen Dinas (Aberystwyth Castle on same site) — Wales
Pencoed — Wales
Pendennis — South-West England
Pendragon — North-West England
Penhow — Wales
Penkill — Scotland
Penmark — Wales
Pennard (Gower Peninsula) (88) — Wales
Penrhyn — Wales
Penrice (Gower Peninsula) — Wales
Penrith — North-West England
Penshurst Place (160) — London & South-East England
Pen-y-Bryn — Wales
Pen-y-Cloddiau Hillfort — Wales
Pen-y-Gaer Hillfort — Wales
Pevensey — London & South-East England
Peveril — Central England
Pickering — North-East England
Picton (199) — Wales
Piel (or Fouldry) (128) — North-West England
Pilsbury — Central England
Pitcon — Scotland
Pitcur — Scotland
Pitreavie — Scotland
Pitsligo — Scotland
Pittairthie — Scotland
Plane Tower — Scotland
Pleshey — Eastern England
Plymouth (Royal Citadel) — South-West England
Plympton — South-West England
Pontefract — North-East England
Popton Fort (Milford Haven) — Wales
Portchester — London & South-East England
Portencross — Scotland
Portland — South-West England
Portsmouth (Round and Square Towers) — London & South-East England
Powderham (140) — South-West England
Powis (194) — Wales
Preston Pele Tower — North-West England
Prudhoe — North-East England
Queenborough — London & South-East England
Queen's Sconce (Newark) — Central England
Queen's View — Scotland
Quenington Knight's Gate — Welsh Marches
Raby (141) — North-East England
Raglan (193) — Wales
Rahoy — Scotland
Rait — Scotland
Randleholme Hall — North-West England
Ravenscraig — Scotland
Ravensworth — North-East England
Rayleigh — Eastern England
Reculver — London & South-East England
Reigate — London & South-East England
Rennibister — Scotland
Restormel (3; 56) — South-West England
Rhuddlan (Castle) (115) — Wales
Ribchester Fort — North-West England
Richard's Castle — Welsh Marches
Richborough (24) — London & South-East England
Richmond (76–7) — North-East England
Ripley (188) — North-East England
Rispain Camp — Scotland
Roch — Wales

Rochester (75) — London & South-East England
Rockingham — Central England
Rosyth — Scotland
Rothesay — Scotland
Rough Castle — Scotland
Rowallan — Scotland
Roxburgh — Scotland
Rumgally House — Scotland
Rumps, The — South-West England
Rushen (Isle of Man) — North-West England
Ruthin — Wales
Ruthven Barracks — Scotland
Rye — London & South-East England
Saddell — Scotland
Saffron Walden — Eastern England
Salcombe — South-West England
Salisbury (Walls of Cathedral Close) — South-West England
Saltwood (158) — London & South-East England
Sandal (Magna) — North-East England
Sandgate — London & South-East England
Sandown (Isle of Wight) — London & South-East England
Sandown (Kent) — London & South-East England
Sandsfoot — South-West England
Scaleby — North-West England
Scarborough (72) — North-East England
Scotney — London & South-East England
Scotstarvit — Scotland
Scoverston Fort — Wales
Scratchbury Hillfort (20–21) — South-West England
Seabegs Wood — Scotland
Sheerness — London & South-East England
Sherborne (New Castle) (181) — South-West England
Sherborne (Old Castle) — South-West England
Sherrif Hutton — North-East England
Shirburn — Central England
Shoreham Old Fort — London & South-East England
Shornemead (Gravesend) — London & South-East England
Shrewsbury — Welsh Marches
Silchester — London & South-East England
Sinclair — Scotland
Sissinghurst (196) — London & South-East England
Sizergh — North-West England
Skelmorlie — Scotland
Skenfrith (74) — Wales
Skibo — Scotland
Skipness — Scotland
Skipsea — North-East England
Skipton — North-East England
Slains — Scotland
Smailholm Tower — Scotland
Snape — North-East England
Sneaton — North-East England
Sodbury Camp Hillfort — Welsh Marches
Sorbie Tower — Scotland
Sorn — Scotland
South Shields (Arbeia) — North-East England
Southampton (Castle and City Walls) — London & South-East England
Southsea — London & South-East England
Spitbank Fort (off Portsmouth) — London & South-East England
Spofforth — North-East England
St Alban's (Verulamium) — Eastern England

St Andrews — Scotland
St Briavels — Welsh Marches
St Catherine's (Fowey) (187) — South-West England
St Conan's Tower — Scotland
St David's (Bishop's Palace) — Wales
St David's (Castle) — Wales
St Donats — Wales
St Helier (see Fort Regent and Castle Elizabeth) —
St Mary's (Isles of Scilly: The Garrison) (183) — South-West England
St Mawes (170–71) — South-West England
St Michael's Mount (130) — South-West England
St Peter Port (see Castle Cornet) —
St Pierre Manor — Wales
Stafford (101) — Central England
Stanwick — North-East England
Star (Isles of Scilly) (182) — South-West England
Stirling — Scotland
Stogursey — South-West England
Stokesay (105) — Welsh Marches
Strathaven — Scotland
Strome — Scotland
Stutfall (see Lympne) —
Sudeley (184–5) — Welsh Marches
Sundrum — Scotland
Sutton Valence — London & South-East England
Swansea — Wales
Tamworth (91) — Central England
Tantallon — Scotland
Tap o'Noth — Scotland
Tarbert — Scotland
Tattershall — Eastern England
Taunton — South-West England
Taymouth — Scotland
Tenby (Castle and Town) (39) — Wales
Terringzean — Scotland
Thetford — Eastern England
Thirlestane — Scotland
Thirlwall — North-East England
Thomaston — Scotland
Thorn Island Fort (Milford Haven) — Wales
Thornbury (195) — Welsh Marches
Thorne — North-East England
Threave — Scotland
Tickhill — North-East England
Tilbury — Eastern England
Tintagel (73) — South-West England
Tiverton — South-West England
Tolquhon — Scotland
Tomen y Rhodwydd — Wales
Tonbridge — London & South-East England
Torksey — Eastern England
Torosay — Scotland
Torr a' Chaisteal — Scotland
Torrisdale — Scotland
Totnes — South-West England
Tower of London (see London, Tower of) —
Trabboch — Scotland
Traprain Law — Scotland
Traquair House — Scotland
Trematon — South-West England
Tre'r Ceiri Hillfort — Wales
Tresco — South-West England
Tretower — Wales
Tullibole — Scotland
Tulloch — Scotland
Turnberry — Scotland
Turton Tower (nr Bolton) — North-West England
Tutbury — Central England
Twt Hill (first Rhuddlan Castle) — Wales
Tynemouth (156–7) — North-East England

Uffington Castle Hillfort (13) — Central England
Upnor (163) — London & South-East England
Urquhart — Scotland
Usk — Wales
Vale (Guernsey) — South-West England
Venlaw — Scotland
Verne Battery (Portland Prison) — South-West England
Vicar's Pele (Corbridge) — North-East England
Vindolanda (or Chesterholm) — North-East England
Walden — Eastern England
Wallingford (Castle and Walls) — London & South-East England
Wallsend (Segedunum) — North-East England
Walmer (166–7) — London & South-East England
Wansdyke (36–7) — South-West England
Wareham (Castle and Walls) — South-West England
Warkworth (Bridge Tower and Castle) (70–71) — North-East England
Warwick (148–9) — Central England
Watling Lodge — Scotland
Wat's Dyke — Welsh Marches
Wattlesborough — Welsh Marches
Wedderburn — Scotland
Weeting — Eastern England
Wells (Bishop's Palace) (150) — South-West England
Welshpool — Wales
Weobley (Gower Peninsula) (143) — Wales
Weoley — Central England
West Blockhouse Battery (Milford Haven) — Wales
West Cowes — London & South-East England
West Malling — London & South-East England
Weymouth — South-West England
Whalley (Abbey Gatehouse) — North-West England
White Castle (or Llantilio) (122) — Wales
White Cathertun — Scotland
White Lea Bastle House — North-West England
Whitley (Epiacum) — North-East England
Whittington — Welsh Marches
Wigmore — Welsh Marches
Wilton — Welsh Marches
Winchelsea — London & South-East England
Winchester (esp. Great Hall) — London & South-East England
Windmill Hillfort (later Royal Fort – Bristol) — South-West England
Windsor (146–7) — London & South-East England
Wingfield — Eastern England
Wiston — Wales
Wolvesey — London & South-East England
Woodsford (Dorset) — South-West England
Woolwich (Arsenal) — London & South-East England
Wray — North-West England
Wraysholme Tower — North-West England
Wressle — North-East England
Wroxeter (35) — Welsh Marches
Yanwath — North-East England
Yarmouth — London & South-East England
Yarnbury — South-West England
York (City Walls and Clifford's Tower) — North-East England

ADDRESSES, ACKNOWLEDGEMENTS AND BIBLIOGRAPHY

USEFUL ADDRESSES AND WEBSITES

Cadw
Welsh Assembly Government
Plas Carew
Unit 5/7 Cefn Coed Parc
Nantgarw
Cardiff CF15 7QQ
Tel: 01443 33 6000
www.cadw.wales.gov.uk

English Heritage
Customer Services Department
PO Box 569
Swindon SN2 2YP
Tel: 0870 333 1181
www.english-heritage.org.uk

Historic Scotland
Longmore House
Salisbury Place
Edinburgh EH9 1SH
Tel: 0131 668 8600
www.historic-scotland.gov.uk

The National Trust for Scotland
Wemyss House
28 Charlotte Square
Edinburgh EH2 4ET
Tel: 0131 243 9300
www.nts.org.uk

The National Trust
Heelis
Kemble Drive
Swindon SN2 2NA
Tel: 0870 458 4000 (membership enquiries)
www.nationaltrust.org.uk

PICTURE ACKNOWLEDGEMENTS

All of the photographs in this book have been licensed from Last Refuge Ltd, with the exception of the images listed below:

pages 6 and 142: jasonhawkes.com

page 18: Crown Copyright: RCAHMS (John Dewar Collection)

pages 50–51: jasonhawkes.com

page 118: © Colin Baxter 2006

page 135: © Crown Copyright: Reproduced courtesy of Historic Scotland

pages 146–7: Skyscan/© Flightimages

page 147: © Skyscan West Photo

page 185: Skyscan/© CLI

page 208: m-satltd/Science Photo Library

FURTHER READING

Armit, Ian, *Towers in the North: The Brochs of Scotland*. Tempus Publishing (2002)

Bede, The Venerable (translated by Bertram Colgrave), *The Ecclesiastical History of the English People*. Oxford Paperbacks (1999)

Blair, Peter Hunter & Keynes, Simon, *An Introduction to Anglo-Saxon England*. Cambridge University Press (2003)

Breeze, David J & Dobson, Brian, *Hadrian's Wall*. Penguin Books (2000)

Brooke, Christopher, *From Alfred to Henry III*. W. W. Norton (1980)

Brown, R. Allen, *English Castles*. The Boydell Press (2004)

Creighton, Oliver, *Castles and Landscapes: Power, Community and Fortification in Medieval England*. Equinox Publishing (2004)

Cunliffe, Barry, *Iron Age Britain*. B. T. Batsford (2004)

Dargie, Richard, *Scottish Castles and Fortifications*. GW Publishing (2004)

Dark, Ken, *Britain and the End of the Roman Empire*. Tempus Publishing (2002)

Darvill, Timothy C., *Prehistoric Britain*. Routledge (1987)

Davies, J., *The King's Ships: Henry VIII and the Birth of the Royal Navy*. Partizan Press (2005)

Douglas, David C., *William the Conqueror*. Yale University Press (1999)

Fraser, Antonia, *Cromwell, Our Chief of Men*. Phoenix Press (2002)

Fry, Plantagenet Somerset, *Castles of Britain and Ireland*. David & Charles (2001)

Gravett, Christopher, *The History of Castles: Fortifications Around the World*. Lyons Press (2001)

Gravett, Christopher & Nicolls, David, *The Normans: Warrior Knights and their Castles*. Osprey (2006)

Hayes, Andrew, *Archaeology of the British Isles: With a Gazetteer of Sites in England, Wales, Scotland and Ireland*. Routledge (1994)

Horspool, David, *Why Alfred Burned the Cakes*. Profile Books (2006)

James, Edward, *Britain in the First Millennium: From Romans to Normans*. Hodder Arnold (2000)

Keen, M. H., *England in the Later Middle Ages*. Routledge (2003)

King, D. J. Cathcart, *The Castle in England and Wales*. Croom Helm (1998)

Kenyon, John R., *Medieval Fortifications*. Leicester University Press (1990)

Lavelle, Ryan (illustrated by Donato Spedaliere & Sarah S. Spedaliere), *Fortifications in Wessex c. 800–1016: The Defences of Alfred the Great against the Vikings*. Osprey (2003)

Liddiard, Robert, *Castles in Context: Power, Symbolism and Landscape, 1066–1500*. Windgather Press (2005)

McAleavy, Tony, *Life in a Medieval Castle*. English Heritage (1998)

Moore, David, *The Welsh Wars of Independence: c. 410–1415*. Tempus Publishing (2004)

Morris, Marc, *Castles: A History of Buildings that Shaped Medieval Britain*. Macmillan (2004)

Norris, John, *Welsh Castles at War*. Tempus Publishing (2004)

Pearson, Michael Parker, *Bronze Age Britain*. B. T. Batsford (2005)

Pettifer, Adrian, *English Castles*. Boydell Press (2002)

Pettifer, Adrian *Welsh Castles*. Boydell Press (2000)

Pryor, Francis, *Farmers in Prehistoric Britain*. Tempus Publishing (1999)

Purkiss, Diane, *The English Civil War: A People's History*. HarperCollins (2006)

Reid, Stuart (illustrated by Graham Turner), *Castles and Tower Houses of the Scottish Clans 1450–1650*. Osprey (2006)

Richards, Julian D., *Viking Age England*. Tempus Publishing (2004)

Ritchie, Anna & Breeze, David J., *Invaders of Scotland: Introduction to the Archaeology of the Romans, Scots, Angles and Vikings*. The Stationery Office Books (1991)

Salter, Mike, *Castles and Tower Houses of Northumberland*. Folly Publications (1997)

Shadrake, Dan & Shadrake, Susanna, *Barbarian Warriors: Saxons, Vikings and Normans*. Brassey's (UK) (1997)

Stenton, Doris Mary, *English Society in the Early Middle Ages*. Penguin Books (1991)

Thompson, M. R., *The Rise of the Castle*. Cambridge University Press (1991)

Toy, Sidney, *Castles: Their Construction and History*. Dover Publications (1985)

Trabraham, Chris, *Scotland's Castles*. B. T. Batsford (2005)

Warner, Philip, *The Medieval Castle: Life in a Fortress in Peace and War*. Penguin Books (2001)

Williams, Geoffrey, *Stronghold Britain*. Sutton Publishing (2003)

Young, Peter & Holmes, Richard, *The English Civil War: A Military History of Three Civil Wars, 1642–1651*. Wordsworth Editions (1999)